WOMEN IN SPACE

....

23 Stories of First Flights, Scientific Missions, and Gravity-Breaking Adventures

KAREN BUSH GIBSON

CHICAGO
REVIEW
PRESS

First hardcover edition published 2014
First paperback edition published 2020
Published by Chicago Review Press Incorporated
814 North Franklin Street
Chicago, Illinois 60610
ISBN 978-1-64160-313-3

The Library of Congress has cataloged the hardcover edition as follows:
Gibson, Karen Bush.
 Women in space : 23 stories of first flights, scientific missions, and gravity-
breaking adventures / Karen Bush Gibson.
 pages cm
 Audience: 12+
 Includes bibliographical references and index.
 ISBN 978-1-61374-844-2 (cloth)
 1. Women astronauts—Biography—Juvenile literature. 2. Women in
astronautics—Juvenile literature. I. Title.

 TL793.G457 2014
 629.450092'52—dc23

 2013024950

Cover and interior design: Sarah Olson
Cover images: (top) Mae Jemison (NASA); (bottom, from left to right) Valentina
Tereshkova (RIA Novasti); Sally Ride (NASA); Sunita Williams (NASA); Liu
Yang (tksteven / Wikipidiacommons)

Printed in the United States of America

To Justus, whose curiosity about space
and life knows no boundaries.

CONTENTS

· · · · · · · · · · · · · · ·

INTRODUCTION

· · · · · · · · · · · · · · · ·

World War II was largely fought and won in the skies with airplanes that flew faster and did more things than ever before. Coming forward as winners from World War II, a modern America began to emerge. A new kind of hero emerged as well—a hero willing to sacrifice self to explore new frontiers. Like the cowboys and pioneers before them, these new heroes had a certain swagger that came from being larger than life. But instead of a ten-gallon hat, the hero wore a space helmet. And like the heroes portrayed in the history books, these new heroes were men.

Astronauts. The first astronauts, those chosen few, experienced what once was only found in science fiction books. Being shot into outer space. Flying in space ships. Going to the moon.

Men made those first journeys. Not that there weren't capable women—there were. American society just wasn't ready . . . or at least those who made the decisions weren't ready. The attitude was that women were to be protected and taken care of, concepts that contradicted becoming astronauts.

The Space Race began soon after the Allies won World War II. America and the former Soviet Union inherited and made use of German technology, specifically rocket technology. Although the two countries had fought on the same side during World War II, their relationship deteriorated in the years afterward. The United States embraced democracy, while the Soviet Union was ruled by communism. Each side possessed nuclear weapons. Though no open battles took place, the United States and the Soviet Union were engaged in a cold war.

Both sides were convinced that their form of government was best. A competition of sorts developed, and the biggest contest was the Space Race. The Soviet Union won the race to be first in space on October 4, 1957, when *Sputnik I* was launched. Weighing in at 184 pounds, *Sputnik I* looked like a metal beach ball with four legs. It orbited the Earth for 98 minutes. Almost a month later, *Sputnik II* went into space carrying a passenger—a dog.

Launching a satellite was something the United States had been working on without much success. One effort exploded on the launch pad. The Soviets' success spurred the United States on, and America had its first success on January 31, 1958. *Explorer I* was launched with a scientific unit that discovered the magnetic radiation belts around the Earth, later known as the Van Allen belts.

The Explorer and Sputnik programs continued with scientific exploration, although both the United States and the Soviet Union still had the occasional failure. Six months after the first Explorer satellite, the US Congress passed the National Aeronautics and Space Act to provide for research into problems of flight within and outside the earth's atmosphere and for other purposes.[1]

Initially, the US Department of Defense oversaw space matters, but President Eisenhower saw the need for a civilian space agency. Many people voiced the opinion that space exploration wasn't a military matter but a scientific one. The National Aeronautics and Space Administration—NASA—was born.

Everyone knew that the next step was putting a person into space. NASA established the Mercury project to reach that goal. President Eisenhower, a five-star army general, decided that astronaut candidates should be selected from a pool of military test pilots. NASA began looking for experienced test pilots with approximately 1,500 hours of flight experience. Hundreds were screened. Groups underwent some of the testing at the Lovelace Medical Clinic and Wright-Patterson Air Force Base.

NASA considered a pilot's strong record of flight experience to be very important. Unlike early Soviet space capsules, which were automated, American spacecraft required experienced pilots at the controls in case of malfunctions. Not having an experienced pilot would have meant death in more than one occasion on the Mercury, Gemini, and Apollo missions.

At a press conference on April 9, 1959, NASA introduced the seven American men who were ready to go into space: Scott Carpenter, Gordon Cooper, John Glenn, Gus Grissom, Walter Schirra, Alan Shepard Jr., and Deke Slayton. With luck, one of them would be the first man in space.

But before that could happen, the Soviets launched *Vostok 1* on April 12, 1961, and Russian cosmonaut Yuri Gagarin became the first person in space. Alan Shepard Jr. followed less than a month later in *Freedom 7*. In the Space Race, the Soviets were still winning.

In the early days of space travel, one consideration in choosing astronauts was weight. Capsule weight, astronaut weight, payload weight—each pound required more fuel, and the fuel added weight as well. Each pound to be launched required three pounds of propellant. Some scientists speculated that more could be done with a lighter load. A woman astronaut would contribute less weight to the capsule, and perhaps this was one contest the United States could win.

When the space program began, women in the United States couldn't get credit cards, rent cars, or obtain loans to buy houses. You didn't see female police officers or professional athletes. When you turned on the television, only male newscasters delivered the nightly news. In the late 1950s, a woman often went from her parents' home to a home with her husband. Some stopped off at college along the way, mainly women's colleges or the few co-ed public colleges that existed. Many private colleges didn't admit women until the 1970s. Princeton and Yale went co-ed in 1969. Dartmouth and Duke allowed women in 1972. Harvard waited until 1977, while Columbia held out until 1983. Today, more than half of college students accepted in any program of higher education are women.

A small minority of women supported themselves, some by performing traditionally male jobs. Pilot Geraldyn "Jerrie" Cobb was an excellent professional pilot by the mid-1950s. But whether she was demonstrating a new airplane or setting a world record, she knew she had to look like a lady. That meant wearing a dress, heels, and lipstick when she climbed into the cockpit.

When women were found who were capable of going into space, the US government said no. NASA was a men-only club with strong government ties. The Soviets, however, said yes and put the first woman in space in 1963. Fifty years ago Valentina Tereshkova became the first woman in space. Nineteen years later, the Soviets would also put the second woman into space.

When the women's movement hit the United States—along with the Civil Rights Act, which prohibited discrimination based on race or gende—things started to change. American

Mission Control Center at Johnson Space Center has provided operational support since the early days of American space flight. *NASA*

women were accepted, even encouraged, into the space program. Sally Ride became the first American woman astronaut thirty years ago. A year later, another woman went up, then another and another. As of 2012, 55 women have been in space, flying shuttles and commanding space stations. Half of NASA's astronaut class of 2013 were women. Many women have been to space multiple times. In 2012, the International Space Station had its second female commander.

These women of courage take on new challenges and adventures. They aren't "women astronauts." Like the men who preceded them, they are astronauts.

The program that opened up opportunities for astronauts, the US space shuttle program, ended in 2011 after thirty years of missions. Astronauts from all nations can still go into space from the Soviet Union, and countries such as China have developed their own space programs.

Still, people wonder what is next for human space exploration. It is still a rare thing for a person to go to space. More people have won lottery jackpots than flown in space.[2]

Private companies are working on different ideas, ranging from space tourism to mining on asteroids. People who have made fortunes from technology—Microsoft, PayPal, Amazon, and Google—are taking the vision that led to their successes and translating it into developing rockets and spaceships. The business of creating commercial rockets and ships is comparable to the early day of developing computers and the Internet.

Space Travelers

Where does the word *astronaut* come from? Astronaut is Greek for "star voyager" or "star sailor." A Belgian science fiction writer, Joseph Henri Honoré Boex, first used the term in 1929, but it didn't become popular until 1961. The Russians prefer to call their space travelers cosmonauts. The first part of that word comes from the Greek word for universe, *kosmos*. Yet *cosmonaut* shares its last syllable with the American term. Whether to the stars or the universe, these space travelers are sailors.

NASA Space Shuttle Program, 1981–2011

....

NASA entered a new age of space exploration with the space shuttle. Reusable spacecraft, named after important ships in history, took people into space to explore, investigate, and build. The first spaceworthy shuttle, *Columbia*, took its first flight on April 12, 1981. The final space shuttle mission ended when the *Atlantis* landed on July 21, 2011. The costs of frequent flights into space were judged to be too high to continue with government-sponsored shuttles. People lined the streets to see the remaining shuttles go to their final homes. The *Endeavour*, the last shuttle built to journey into space, journeyed on land to the California Science Center in Los Angeles.

Enterprise: Named after the spaceship in *Star Trek*; used only in testing.

Columbia: Named after one of the first ships to sail around the world.

Challenger: Named after a navy ship that explored the Atlantic and Pacific oceans from 1872 to 1876.

Discovery: Named after two ships—the vessel Henry Hudson used in discovering Hudson Bay and one used by Captain James Cook to explore Hawaii, Alaska, and Canada.

Atlantis: Named after a boat that sailed more than a half million miles in more than 30 years of ocean research.

Endeavour: Named after the first ship of explorer Captain Cook, who sailed through the world in the late 18th century; suggested by schoolchildren.

WOMEN WHO HAVE BEEN TO SPACE

· ·

Anousheh Ansari

Ellen S. Baker*

Roberta Bondar

Kalpana Chawla*

Laurel Clark

Mary L. Cleave

Catherine G. Coleman*

Eileen M. Collins*

Nancy Jane Currie*

N. Jan Davis*

Bonnie J. Dunbar*

Tracy E. Caldwell Dyson*

Anna L. Fisher

Linda M. Godwin*

Susan J. Helms*

Joan Higginbotham

Kathryn P. Hire

Millie Hughes-Fulford

Claudie André-Deshays
  Haigneré*

Marsha S. Ivins*

Mae C. Jemison

Tamara E. Jernigan*

Janet L. Kavandi*

Elena V. Kondakova*

Wendy B. Lawrence*

Pamela A. Melroy*

Dorothy Metcalf-Lindenburger

Shannon W. Lucid*

Sandra H. Magnus*

K. Megan McArthur

Barbara R. Morgan

Chiaki Mukai*

Lisa M. Nowak

Karen L. Nyberg*

Ellen Ochoa*

Julie Payette*

Judith A. Resnik

Sally K. Ride*

M. Rhea Seddon*

Svetlana Savitskaya*

Helen Sharman

Nancy J. Currie

Yi Soyeon

Heidemarie M.
  Stefanyshyn-Piper*

Susan L. Still*

Nicole P. Stott*

Kathryn D. Sullivan*

Kathryn C. Thornton*

Valentina Tereshkova

Janice E. Voss*

Shannon Walker

Mary Ellen Weber*

Peggy Whitson*

Sunita Williams*

Stephanie D. Wilson*

Naoko Yamazaki

Liu Yang

*More than one flight to space

PART I

....

THE MERCURY 13

Like universities across the country, the University of Wisconsin–Oshkosh holds its spring commencement in May. In addition to celebrating the year's graduates, the school, like many colleges, recognizes special people by awarding them with honorary doctorates. In 2007, the University of Wisconsin conferred doctorates on 13 women who showed their determination, strength, and bravery in the Space Race with accomplishments that paved the way for generations.[1]

Many Americans have heard of the Mercury 7. When America's first seven astronauts were announced, their confident, smiling faces appeared on television and on magazine covers. Later, these seven test pilots were further immortalized in the book *The Right Stuff* by Tom Wolfe and in the award-winning 1983 movie of the same name. But have you heard of the Mercury 13? Many people haven't. When the University of Wisconsin–Oshkosh honored the Mercury 13, the event made news because the story had been kept fairly quiet for almost 50 years.

The Mercury 13 were America's first women astronauts. According ABC News correspondent Natalie Arnold, who covered the story, the Mercury 13 are the women our country didn't want anyone to know about.[2]

In truth, even the name Mercury 13 was relatively new. For more than 30 years, these women weren't known as anything other than who they were. But the 13 women were some of the best pilots in the world in the early 1960s. They underwent the same tests and indignities that the original Mercury 7 went through, and more. And they passed. Some of them even *exceeded* the performance of the male astronauts. Several of the women let themselves hope that they, too, would get to show their "right stuff" and fly into space.

If Americans ever knew, many of them forgot that these women had taken part in astronaut testing in the early 1960s. Others tried to sweep the brief flirtation that America had with women astronauts under the rug. But the story refused to die. Along the way, people began to refer to the group as the "Mercury 13."

Although some of the women knew each other, most did not meet until 1986, when Bernice "B" Steadman decided to hold a 25th anniversary get-together. Not everyone came, but enough women came to find that they had a bond that would last throughout time.

In 1994, Gene Nora Jessen tried again. A former president of the Ninety-Nines, Inc., International Organization of Women Pilots, she tracked everyone down through their memberships in the Ninety-Nines. This gathering at the group's headquarters in Oklahoma City wouldn't be just for remembering; it would also be about celebrating the fact that a woman pilot—Eileen Collins—would finally be flying a ship into space.

Gene Nora invited Eileen, as well. She met the women, listened to their stories, and thanked them. Nine of the thirteen women attended the banquet. Jerrie Cobb arrived late, flying in from the Amazon. Seven of the women attended Eileen's first launch as pilot the following year. Eight of the Mercury 13 arrived for the launch when Eileen became the first commander of a spaceflight in 1999.

In 2004, journalist Martha Ackmann published *The Mercury 13: The True Story of Thirteen Women and the Dream of Space Flight.* The book received a lot of attention. Television news shows publicized the book and the women. Newspapers did interviews with several of the women, and a few other books followed, as well.

The Oshkosh campus, one of 20 under the University of Wisconsin umbrella, started as a teachers' college. It had long been a leader in education, establishing one of the first kindergartens and introducing practice teaching to further the studies of its students. Each year, the university holds a program for freshmen known as Odyssey, in which students explore social justice issues. In 2007, freshmen students met author Martha Ackmann and pilot Mary Wallace "Wally" Funk. It was a tale that begged to be told, and so the story of the Mercury 13 spread all over campus, inspiring everyone who heard it.

Convinced that the 13 women deserved more than a brief blitz of media attention, the University of Wisconsin–Oshkosh decided to honor the Mercury 13 in 2007. Once the commencement was scheduled, the word went out. Newspapers from San Francisco to Miami covered the Mercury 13. The Associated Press picked up the story, and it was published in 43 states. News channels CNN and Fox News provided coverage, as did CBS News and National Public Radio. It spread outside the United States as well, to eight countries and five continents.

The event started on Friday, May 11, with a panel discussion with the Mercury 13 women. Martha Ackmann served as moderator and, along with the eight women who could attend, told the story. Jerrie Cobb, in her trademark ponytail, said more than once that she still planned to go into space. When she acknowledged that the recognition by the University of Wisconsin was the first they had received, the audience gave the women a standing ovation.

The following morning they received honorary doctor of science degrees for their pioneering spirit. Dr. Steven Kagen, a congressman from Wisconsin, presented them with their degrees. Less than a month later, the US House of Representatives approved House Resolution 421 to honor the Mercury 13 for their service. Sponsored by Kagen, the resolution recognized the accomplishments of the 13 women who outshined and outperformed their male counterparts—but were never allowed to fly into space.[3]

THE ASTRONAUTS
WHO NEVER WERE

....

The space capsule shot deep into the water, turning upside down on its journey. Jerrie Cobb looked around and saw the cockpit filling up with water. Undoing her seat belt, she went to the top of the capsule, now facing down as the water gurgled in. She tried not to think of the extra weight she carried—the parachute pack and the inflatable life jacket over her clothing. Jerrie moved carefully in the close confines of the capsule. Time was of the essence—she was now completely underwater—and she didn't want her pack or any part of her getting hung up on the controls.

Jerrie Cobb in the MASTIF or Multiple Axis Space Test Inertia Facility, which was used to train astronauts to control a spinning spacecraft. *NASA*

Easing out of the capsule, she began swimming immediately. When she broke the surface of the water, men in diving suits were there. She had saved them a trip to the bottom of the pool because she had conquered the Dilbert Dunker, a water survival test for astronaut candidates. Like some of the other testing in the third and final phase of tests, the Dilbert Dunker could only be found at the Naval Air Station Pensacola in Florida.

She also found herself being fired from a cockpit in an ejection seat, throwing darts and tennis balls at a target in a constantly revolving room, and soaring to an altitude of 60,000 feet to test her flying skills while wearing a full-pressure suit. She had also flown as a passenger in a navy fighter jet—with 18 needles in her head so that her reactions to shifting gravity could be measured as the plane made loops, rolls, and dives.

Dr. R. A. Carleton, a cardiologist and navy officer in the Navy Medical Corps, had already observed Jerrie through a two-day physical and a physical fitness test. He couldn't help but admire her determination. The physical fitness test was set up for subjects taller, heavier, and with a greater muscle mass—in other words, men. Still, Jerrie did her best. When asked to do 30 sit-ups, she did 42. Although she was a former softball player who had wrestled the controls in airplanes in the worst weather conditions, she could not pull her body weight up to the chin-up bar. But when asked to scale a wall a foot taller than her five-foot-seven frame, she made it on the second try.

When the Pensacola tests were complete, she had passed. There were no more tests, only admission to astronaut training. For two years, she had gone through every test imaginable and passed them all. She knew she wasn't the only one. Twelve more women would be arriving in Pensacola in a few weeks to undergo the same tests she had. They were ready for Phase III of the "girl astronaut program."

No doubt, Jerrie often thought back to that chance walk on a Miami beach in the fall of 1959. Part of her job at Aero Design and Engineering, an aircraft manufacturer, was flying at conventions to interest potential buyers in the company's airplanes. As Jerrie and her boss, Tom Harris, talked before that day's events at the Air Force Association conference, two men who had just had a swim in the ocean were headed in their direction. She didn't know them, but Tom did. He introduced Jerrie to Dr. William Randolph Lovelace II and Brigadier General Donald Flickinger. The two men had recently been to the Soviet Union, where the talk was that the Russians were considering sending a woman into space. The idea interested both men immensely.

After the introductions, Lovelace and Flickinger said something about an airplane the Soviets were testing. Jerrie, who often hung back in conversations due to her shyness, spoke up with her opinion about the plane, which the Soviets had been having trouble with. Airplanes, after all, were something she knew about. Her intelligent comment caused the two men to ask if she was a pilot.

When this young woman of 28 explained that she had been flying for 16 years, Lovelace and Flickinger found it hard to believe. When her father had taken her for a ride at age 12 in a rebuilt, open-cockpit Waco biplane, she had fallen in love with flying. She repeatedly asked for lessons. After Jerrie promised to bring her grades up in school, her parents agreed. Her father taught her informally until she was old enough for professional lessons. On her birthdays, she would test for whatever license she was finally old enough to have. At 16, she received her private pilot's license. When she reached 18, it was a commercial license; two years later, she also had a flight instructor rating and an instrument rating.

After trying college for a year, she earned money for her own airplane by playing softball. Jerrie was ready for a career in aviation, but the problem was that nobody wanted to hire a woman pilot. She finally got a job ferrying aircraft, including military planes, to South America. It was a dangerous job with long flights and hazardous conditions. One flight landed her in jail when she touched down in Ecuador with a military bomber meant for Peru. She loved her job. After performing that hazardous job for a few years and setting some aviation records, her career options began to open up.

The two men invited Jerrie back to the Fontainebleau Hotel to talk. Lovelace was a respected physician who had focused his career on aviation medicine after training at the Mayo Clinic. He was particularly interested in medical issues involving advanced aircraft, such as the oxygen deprivation that occurs at high altitudes. Lovelace also designed the tests that the Mercury 7 astronauts had gone through at his Albuquerque clinic.

General Flickinger, trained as a surgeon, was a war hero who parachuted to plane crash sites to offer medical aid during World War II. In 1959, Flickinger served as director of research for the Air Force Air Research and Development Command.

The men told Jerrie about Project WISE (Women in Space Earliest), a proposal Flickinger wanted the air force to pursue. He had already approached NASA about it, but they had turned him down. The prevailing medical and scientific opinion of the day was that menstruation caused changes in the brain, such as being distractible and emotional and not thinking clearly. This would make women incapable of safely piloting airplanes, jets, or spacecraft. Women who had served as Women Airforce Service Pilots (WASPs) during World War II had been grounded— not allowed to fly—when supervisors knew they were on their periods. The women pilots soon learned to keep this information to themselves, and their accident rate was less than that of their male counterparts.

Flickinger, referring to Project WISE as the "girl astronaut program," wanted to evaluate how female pilots did on the Project Mercury tests. Earlier research had already demonstrated that women tended to respond better to withstanding pain, loneliness, and extreme temperatures. Would Jerrie be interested in participating in the project? he asked.

Astronaut testing? Jerrie didn't even have to think about it. As one of the world's top pilots, she knew that the next aviation frontier was space. She agreed immediately. The men swore her to secrecy and told her they would be in touch.

Did Jerrie know that she was being checked out? If so, she probably didn't care. As winner of both the Woman of the Year in Aviation and Pilot of the Year awards from the Women's National Aeronautic Association and the National Pilots Association, she had logged more than 7,000 flight hours and established three world records: altitude, distance, and speed. She was also one of the few pilots to have received the Fédération Aéronautique Internationale (FAI) Gold Wings of Achievement. Some said she was the best female pilot in the world.

Jerrie returned to Oklahoma and her job as a pilot-manager at Aero Design. The one high point of the months of waiting came when Tyndall Air Force Base honored her aviation skills and honors by letting her fly a military jet, the Delta Dagger TF-102A. She not only got to fly the jet—she broke the sound barrier in it.

Each day she went to her mailbox, hoping to find a letter from Lovelace. The letter finally arrived around Christmas. She was approved for the program! She was to report to Dr. Lovelace's clinic in February. She got busy training. Jerrie wanted to be in the best shape possible when they started the Mercury tests on her.

She ran in the morning before work, usually barefoot, in a vacant lot across the street from her home. Often she ran laps when she returned from work too. Soon she was running five miles a day and riding a stationary bike for another 20 miles. Sometimes she swam or played tennis or golf as well. She also ate protein-filled meals, including hamburgers for breakfast.

There had been another development with Flickinger's "girl astronaut program" as well. Before meeting Jerrie, he had arranged for aviation pioneer Ruth Nichols to undergo testing at the Aero Medical Laboratory at Wright-Patterson Air Force Base in Dayton, Ohio. At 58, Nichols was considered too old for the space program—by everyone but herself. Nichols went through three days of tests; many were tests Jerrie would go through in Albuquerque, New Mexico. Others, like the centrifuge, weren't readily available.

For any age, Nichols performed quite well on the tests. Anyone who knew Ruth knew that her determination to succeed was phenomenal. Nichols later told people that when she suggested that air force personnel use her test information to put a woman in space, they said, "Under no circumstances."[1] They had only wanted to gather data about how women did in testing.

Not willing to give up, Nichols told people about the testing. When the testing was made public, the air force was afraid the publicity connected to women in astronaut training would damage the air force's reputation. Flickinger was told to pull the plug on the program. With Flickinger and the air force out of the picture, Lovelace was forced to either abandon the project or continue it privately. He chose to continue with what he referred to as the "Woman in Space Program" in letters to potential candidates.

Jerrie arrived in Albuquerque on Valentine's Day. She reported to the clinic the next day for the most thorough medical evaluation she had ever had. She was poked more times that she could count, and the X-rays soon numbered about a

Ruth Nichols

Ruth Nichols began flying airplanes as a teenager and even became the first woman licensed to fly a seaplane. During her life, she flew more than 140 different types of airplanes, setting records for altitude, distance, and speed. She even got the chance to fly a military jet when her brother, an air force colonel, pulled some strings. Ruth often competed against Amelia Earhart and sometimes beat her. When flying opportunities for women dried up after World War II, Ruth was frustrated but began to think that perhaps space would offer women new flying opportunities.

Ruth participated in tests for three days. She tested in a flight simulator, easily conquering it. She was also tested in weightlessness and the centrifuge. The centrifuge was like a roller coaster that she had to control. The most difficult test, in her opinion, was the isolation chamber where she remained in total darkness.

When it was over, Ruth continued to hope that, in some way, she would be allowed to be an astronaut. But the air force, which was the agency charged with space exploration in the late 1950s, refused to consider any woman for astronaut training. Slightly more than a year after astronaut testing, Nichols was found dead in her apartment. Suicide was determined to be the cause of death.

hundred. Strapped to a table that tilted back and forth, her heart functions were measured for 30 minutes. She pedaled on an exercise bicycle programmed for increasingly steeper hills to the point of exhaustion. Jerrie called it her "bicycle ride toward space."[2]

By far the most uncomfortable test she had to endure was having icy water poured into her ear canal. "Almost immediately, the ceiling began to whirl and became a multiple of spinning blobs," Jerrie recalled.[3] Ice water attacks the sense of balance and causes extreme dizziness in everyone. Doctors wanted to know how long it took a candidate to regain balance.

After a week of testing, flight surgeon Robert Secrest told Jerrie that not only had she passed, but she had scored in the top 2 percent of all astronaut test candidates. She was ready for Phase II of the testing. But Lovelace wanted to see if other women would pass the tests or whether Jerrie was in a class by herself. He needed to test more female pilots.

In all, Lovelace invited 25 more women to test. Jerrie had provided him with some names that she had pulled from the Ninety-Nines membership rolls. She recommended women like Betty Skelton, who had also been through some privately funded astronaut testing, and acquaintances like Jerri Sloan, a Texas aviator who had been in many flying competitions with Jerrie.

Meanwhile, Lovelace was preparing to release the results of Jerrie's testing at the Space and Naval Congress, which was attended by world experts and aviation doctors. Almost a year after meeting Jerrie on the beach, he was telling other medical and space professionals, "We are already in a position to say that certain qualities of the female space pilot are preferable to those of her male colleague."[4]

Women better astronauts than men? This was news. *Life* magazine had gotten the scoop, making a deal with Lovelace for exclusive rights to the story. *Life* released the story and pictures from the testing as soon as Lovelace made the announcement.

Astronauts were big business, particularly since American Alan Shepard had been launched into space on May 5, 1961, three weeks after Soviet cosmonaut Yuri Gagarin. Later that month, President Kennedy had announced to the nation that the United States would have a man on the moon by the end of the 1960s. America had space fever.

Between the *Life* magazine coverage and Lovelace stating that women just might be better astronauts, there was an explosion of interest in women in space, and particularly the first potential female astronaut, Jerrie Cobb. Many newspapers treated it as front-page news—the *Washington Post* ran a story titled "Woman Qualifies for Space Training" on August 19, 1960.

Jerrie became an instant celebrity. Reporters called the homes of her family and friends to track Jerrie down. In their stories, they called her everything—astro-nette, feminaut, astronautrix, and space girl. Focusing on Jerrie's blonde ponytail and freckles, the media wrote about the "girl" who would fly into space, not the accomplished pilot. One of the phrases used to refer to Jerrie was "first lady astronaut." Jerrie adopted the term, but put her own spin on it, referring to herself and the other women testers as fellow or first lady astronaut trainees (FLATs).

Shy Jerrie was overwhelmed by the attention, but she was smart enough to know that positive publicity would help the cause. She submitted to interviews and press events. Jerrie answered every question they threw at her, even though many had nothing to do with flying into space, such as what she liked to cook. She even responded to ridiculous questions like an inquiry about her physical measurements by *Time* magazine.

"Aren't you afraid of going into space?" asked one reporter.

Betty Skelton

Quite simply, Betty Skelton was a woman who loved speed, whether it was by air or land. Skelton used to watch the navy pilots from her home in Pensacola when she was eight years old. Taking her first solo flight at 12 (although it was not legal), she soon became an aerobatic flyer known for her "inverted ribbon cut." The maneuvers had her flying an open-cockpit biplane upside down about 10 feet above the ground and slicing through a ribbon stretched between two poles. She won the United States Feminine Aerobatic Championship three years in a row. And by the late 1950s, she was setting land-speed records with racecars. She eventually set 17 aviation and auto records.

When Skelton appeared on the cover of *Look* magazine in a silver astronaut's flight suit in 1960, it was the first time that people began talking publicly about women astronauts. The headline read, "Should a Girl Be First in Space?"

With the growing American interest in flying and space, *Look* was one of several magazines that had an aviation editor. That editor invited Skelton to take part in astronaut testing with the cooperation of NASA, the air force, and the navy. *Look* magazine wanted to compete against its chief publishing rival, *Life*, which had paid a half million dollars for the exclusive rights to the story of the Mercury 7 project.

(continued on the next page)

Although her testing was designed to be little more than publicity for the magazine and good public relations for NASA and the military, Skelton did perform tests in several areas, including the tilt table and weightlessness. She reportedly did well. Although she did not aspire to be an astronaut, she knew it was something women could do. Betty said, "I felt it was an opportunity to try to convince them that a woman could do this type of thing and could do it well."[5]

Unfortunately, her results weren't included in the article. Instead, the petite pilot and racecar driver was photographed in men's pajamas taking advice from Mercury 7 astronauts, who dubbed her "7½." The magazine did provide characteristics of the future female astronauts: under 35, married, flat-chested, and athletic. Although she should be a pilot with a range of scientific knowledge, the article suggested she would be brought on a spaceflight as a "scientist-wife."

"No, I'm looking forward to that opportunity," Jerrie answered.

"What are you afraid of?"

"Grasshoppers," she quickly answered, knowing a response was required.[6]

Most of all, she let everyone know that she wasn't trying to replace the male astronauts. She just wanted to be part of the space program.

As soon as she could, Jerrie escaped back to Oklahoma to return to work and await the second phase of testing. She thought a lot about flying in space. Since meeting Flickinger and Lovelace, it had become all she could think about.

Meanwhile, Lovelace found the costs of the testing prohibitive, particularly without government funding. He turned to his old friend, Jackie Cochran, and her husband, Floyd Odlum. Odlum chaired the board of the Lovelace Foundation. He and his wife had given millions to the clinic over the years. Additionally, Jackie Cochran was a phenomenal pilot and one of the few women who saw her flying reputation soar after World War II, when most of the WASPs that she trained and supervised during the war couldn't find jobs as pilots.

Jackie was one of the only American women to fly military jets and had even been the first woman to break the sound barrier—flying faster than the speed known as Mach 1—in 1953. The second woman to break the sound barrier was one of Cochran's WASPs, Jean Hixson, who flew a Delta Dagger military jet in 1958, which was against regulations. Jean Hixson was also became a candidate for astronaut testing.

While Jackie was happy to help Lovelace, whom she had recommended to President Franklin D. Roosevelt for a top aviation award, she was also used to being the top female pilot and having the publicity. Now, she wasn't the center of attention. The focus was instead on Jerrie Cobb.

Women like Cobb, Cochran, and Nichols understood that space was the next challenge for pilots. Jackie Cochran may have thought that she was the obvious choice as the first female astronaut. But she was already in her 50s, and she had been diagnosed with a heart condition. Sarah Gorelick, one of the women being tested, overheard Cochran and Lovelace in a shouting match over Cochran doing the tests. Lovelace stood firm. Jackie Cochran would not be one of the test candidates.

If she couldn't be the top astronaut candidate, Jackie decided she would be in charge. In addition to becoming the public voice of the program, Jackie began her own recruiting and submitted 11 names for testing, including twin pilots Jan and Marion Dietrich. On April 30, 1961, the twins appeared in an article for *Parade* magazine, "Jan and Marion Dietrich: First Astronaut Twins." The author was Jackie Cochran. Lovelace didn't care about publicity. He was a scientist first; he just wanted to test the women.

One of the 25 invitations that Lovelace mailed went to 20-year-old Mary Wallace Funk. Known as Wally, she was a flight instructor at Fort Sill, an army base in southwestern Oklahoma, when she picked up the *Life* magazine featuring Jerrie Cobb. After graduating from Oklahoma State University as the Flying Aggies' top female pilot, Wally had gotten a job teaching military men how to fly. When she saw the article about women flying in space, she knew this was something she had to do. She quickly wrote to Lovelace and volunteered. Impressed by the experience of someone so young, Lovelace sent her an invitation, but her mother had to give Wally permission due to her age.

Gene Nora Stumbough, a flying instructor at the University of Oklahoma, heard about the astronaut testing from Wally Funk at an Oklahoma college aviation gathering. She immediately wrote to Dr. Lovelace to tell him that he couldn't possibly do the testing without her. After she detailed her flight experience, he agreed and sent an invitation.

Of the 25 invited, 19 women journeyed to Albuquerque. They ranged in age from 21 (Wally, who had celebrated a birthday since receiving her invitation) to 40. Some were single; others were married. They came from all walks of life. What they had in common was that they were all expert pilots with at least a commercial rating and more than 2,000 hours of flying time.

Lovelace had also tested the Mercury 7, but the government came up with the criteria for that testing. For the Mercury 7 project, men had to be military test pilots, each with at least

Astronaut Qualifications

••

Astronaut requirements for NASA have changed through the years, although things like excellent health remain important. Age is no longer a consideration, although most have started the program between 26 and 46 years of age. Here are some of today's requirements for NASA astronauts:

1. US citizenship.

2. Bachelor's degree from an accredited institution. Degree should be in engineering, biological science, physical science, or math.

3. Three years of post-degree professional experience. A master's degree can substitute for one year; a doctoral degree can replace all three years.

4. If a candidate does not have the professional experience listed above, he or she must have at least 1,000 pilot-in-command hours in a jet aircraft.

5. Must be able to pass a NASA long-duration space flight physical with blood pressure under 140/90.

6. Visual acuity correctable to 20/20; if there have been surgical procedures to the eye, such as LASIK, a year must have passed since the latest procedure.

7. Height between 62 and 75 inches.

1,500 hours flight experience and a bachelor's degree in engineering. They also had to be less than 40 years old, less than 5 foot 11, and in excellent physical condition. The height requirement was due to the small size of the capsules.

The women checked into the Bird of Paradise Motel across from the pueblo-style building that housed the Lovelace Clinic on Gibson Boulevard. They were scheduled for testing one or two at a time. It would be many years before they all met one another, although those with testing partners got to know their partners well. Jerri Sloan and Bernice Steadman, who went by "B," shared many uncomfortable testing moments and even more laughs. B Steadman, the owner of an aviation business in Michigan, suggested Jane Hart for consideration.

Jane "Janey" Hart, the mother of eight children and wife of a senator, shared her testing with Gene Nora Stumbough.

At the age of 24, Gene Nora hadn't been out of college long, and she was a little intimidated by her 40-year-old partner. Janey, a personable woman who spoke her mind, soon set Gene Nora at ease, and they became lifelong friends.

Flight crew prepares the Mercury 8 capsule for astronaut Wally Schirra's flight. *NASA*

Appointments started around 8 AM, sometimes earlier, each morning for a week. The first day began with a complete medical and aviation history, followed by a comprehensive check-up by an internist or flight surgeon. Blood and lab tests followed, including more than 100 X-rays of each woman. Once the women thought that there was nothing else to do, there would be even more tests. Every part of their bodies was checked. More than a dozen eye tests were performed. At the time, only a couple men had been to space and just for very short periods of time. No one knew what was important in a medical history, so the doctors performed every test possible.

With the women strapped to tilt tables with their heads angled down at 65 degrees, a cardiologist checked their heart functions as an electrocardiogram recorded information every five minutes.

Covered in sensors, the women pedaled an exercise bike in time to a metronome. Every minute, the medical staff added drag to the back wheel until each woman's pulse reached 180. Sweat dripped into their eyes until they burned. As the women biked past the point of exhaustion, doctors measured the oxygen they were taking in and the carbon dioxide they were breathing out.

Many of the tests were uncomfortable or grueling. Each woman swallowed a rubber tube so that doctors could test her stomach acids, and her reflexes were tested by electric shocks applied to her arms. And like Jerrie, no one enjoyed the inner ear function test.

One day involved being flown to Los Alamos and then traveling below ground for the tests. The women arrived in a small room and climbed into a small tube, called a nuclear counter, that provided little room to move. The test had two purposes. In addition to calculating lean body mass, the testing situation also checked for claustrophobia since space capsules were quite small. There was a "chicken switch" in the testing chamber for the candidates to flip if they wanted to come out early; a couple of the women took advantage of it.

Dr. Donald Kilgore with the Lovelace Foundation reported that the women performed well and complained far less than the men did. "I think women are more tolerant of pain and discomfort than men anyhow," he said.[7]

The women did not learn whether they had passed until after they returned home. Those who passed received a letter from Randy Lovelace congratulating them and asking if they were interested in continuing with the next phase of testing. All answered yes.

Twelve more women had passed Phase I of the testing around the time Jerrie Cobb finished Phrase II. She didn't have to travel far for the next phase of testing, just to the Oklahoma City VA Medical Center. Wright-Patterson Air Force Base had refused to allow further testing on women astronaut candidates for fear that the public would think they advocated women in space.

Jerrie took various psychological examinations—IQ tests, sentence completion and draw-a-person exercises, and the Minnesota Multiphasic Personality Inventory (MMPI). She even told the examiners what she thought the inkblots on the Rorschach tests looked like. What she found most difficult was talking about a personal experience for five minutes. A speech impediment, which she'd had since childhood, had led to a dislike of speaking in front of others. Long ago, Jerrie determined she wasn't a talker; she was a doer.

While the psychological testing provided more information to Lovelace, the exams were also a way to screen people for the sensory deprivation test. It was an experience some people weren't able to cope with. In fact, it had led to hallucinations in about half the people tested.

After passing her psychological exams, Jerrie was told to go home and get a good night's sleep. When she returned to the hospital the next day, she put on a swimsuit and entered the sensory deprivation chamber.

At the time, sensory deprivation testing was still evolving. Early testing, including with the Mercury 7 men, had taken place in dark rooms with a chair and table for two to three hours. During John Glenn's test, he found pencil and paper and wrote 18 pages to keep himself occupied. Psychiatrist Dr. Jay Shurley felt those tests were inadequate to test for true sensory deprivation.

The sensory deprivation chamber that Jerrie tested in contained a pool surrounded by eight-inch steel walls. Both the water and the air were exactly the same temperature as her body. Not only would she not be able to see or hear anything but her own voice, she also wouldn't be able to feel anything.

The staff strapped Jerrie in so that she was suspended in the water. Although the staff explained that they couldn't talk back to her, she was welcome to talk. She could be released whenever she wanted; she just had to tell them. When they shut the door, the darkness was complete. There was never any point when the eyes became adjusted to the dark so that she could see. There was nothing—no sound, vision, or feeling.

Jerrie described the experience as very relaxing. Between her job and the testing, she was often on the go. She might have slept awhile; she wasn't certain. Occasionally, she would speak out and let the examiners know that everything was all right. She was peaceful and relaxed. Finally, she announced that she was ready to get out, although she added that she could stay longer.

When Jerrie was helped out of the sensory deprivation tank, the examiners asked her how long she thought she had been in. "I don't know, maybe six or seven hours," she said.[8] They showed Jerrie a clock. She had been in for 9 hours and 40 minutes, longer than anyone had ever experienced.

Dr. Shurley reported to Lovelace that Jerrie Cobb had high motivation to become an astronaut. Flying was everything to her. She possessed exceptional if not unique qualities for serving as an astronaut.[9]

Jerrie wanted the other women to succeed as well in order to prove that she wasn't a fluke. She invited the others to Oklahoma City for the second phase of testing, offering her home as a place they could stay. While most decided to wait for the Pensacola tests, two women—Rhea Hurrle and Wally Funk—took Jerrie up on her offer.

If the staff had been impressed with Jerrie, they may not have known what to make of Rhea and Wally. Rhea arrived a few days before Wally. During her time in the tank, she spoke and moved little, only offering the occasional observation. She did not ask to come out, but was pulled out of the chamber at ten hours. A few days later, Wally took her turn. During her entire time in the tank, she did not say one word. She also was removed from the tank without asking, at 10 hours and 35 minutes.

The momentum behind putting a woman in space was building, but NASA remained quiet and uninvolved. At a speaking event, Jerrie Cobb found herself sitting next to the head of NASA, James Webb. When Webb got up to speak, he announced that Jerrie Cobb had been named a consultant for NASA. No one was more surprised than Jerrie, and the announcement fueled her belief that she would someday go into space. She began writing letters and memos to NASA to keep them informed of her progress in testing.

When Jerrie finished the last of the testing at Pensacola, she sent a letter to Webb about completing the tests successfully. The plan was that seven more of the successful women candidates would also fly to the naval station to take part in the same tests, including the g-force and high-altitude testing.

Two women, Sarah Gorelick and Gene Nora Stumbough, had to quit their jobs in order to continue testing. It was a difficult decision to make, but the chance to be an astronaut was not an opportunity that came every day.

In September 1961, a few days before the Pensacola phase was to begin, Lovelace sent telegrams to the women scheduled to arrive for testing. Gene Nora opened her telegram, expecting perhaps more instructions or even confirming the test dates. Instead, the telegram said:

> Regret to advise arrangements at Pensacola canceled. Probably will not be possible. You may return expense advance to Lovelace Foundation c/o me. Letter will advise of additional developments when matter cleared further.[10]

What had happened? The official story was that the naval base had learned there was no official request from NASA for the testing. Without proper authorization, the navy had canceled the tests. NASA responded that there had never been an official women's astronaut program.

The women of the Mercury 13 were stunned. Jerrie Cobb and Janey Hart flew into action. Janey, the wife of Michigan senator Philip Hart, was familiar with the workings of Washington, DC, and she knew many of the big names in government. Janey wrote to each member of the House Committee on Science and Aeronautics. She spoke with congressional leaders about resuming testing. She and Jerrie wrote to President Kennedy. And they found an ally in Liz Carpenter, the assistant of Vice President Lyndon Johnson.

After talking with the women, Carpenter drafted a letter to NASA from Johnson asking whether anyone had been disqualified from astronaut testing because of being a woman. Instead of approving and signing the letter, Johnson wrote across the top, "Let's stop this now."[11]

When Jerrie and Janey met with Vice President Johnson, he gave the women five minutes to speak before telling them that there was nothing he could do. It had been Johnson, as a senator in the late 1950s, who had pushed the Space Race. When elected vice president, he was put in charge of the space program. This was a man who had the power to change things—but he didn't. Jerrie later shared what Johnson had told her: "Jerrie, if we let you or other women into the space program, we have to let blacks in, we'd have to let Mexican-Americans in, we have to let every minority in and we just can't do it."[12]

People began asking Representative George Miller, chairman of the House Committee on Science and Astronautics, about women astronauts. He told the media about the "very vocal group of women" who thought there should be women astronauts and agreed that "a woman astronaut would eventually be put into orbit around the earth."[13]

But Miller hadn't said *when* there would be women astronauts. A special subcommittee hearing of the House Committee on Science and Aeronautics was scheduled to determine whether the women had been discriminated against due to their gender. The hearing was held two years before the Civil Rights Act was passed. Even if it was determined that gender discrimination had occurred, that wasn't against the law yet. However, people were already discussing racial and gender discrimination.

Representative Victor Anfuso of New York called the hearing to order on Tuesday, July 17, 1962. "Ladies and gentlemen, we meet this morning to consider the very important problem of determining the basic qualifications required for the selection and training of astronauts."[14] Anfuso welcomed Jerrie Cobb and Janey Hart, who were representing the Mercury 13. Janey Hart discussed how 100 years earlier, men served as hospital attendants and women were thought of as too weak to withstand the horrors of military hospitals. Yet women insisted they could do the job, and when there was a shortage of men to do the work, women did it successfully. These were the first nurses. She compared that to the situation with astronauts.

Jerrie shared the story of passing the Mercury astronaut tests. She even showed pictures of the testing and explained how other women had been tested. She talked about the benefits of using women in the space program. Nervous about talking to congressmen, she kept flipping her shoes off under the table. Unfortunately, a photographer caught her without her shoes. More attention was paid to that photo than to the reason for the hearing.

"I'm not arguing that women be admitted to space merely so they won't feel discriminated against. I am arguing that they be admitted because they have a real contribution to make,"[15] Janey Hart told the committee.

Jackie Cochran was called to speak. If Janey and Jerrie thought that a fellow woman pilot and the person who had helped fund their testing would speak up for the Mercury 13, they were in for a shock. Instead, Cochran told the committee that a special program for training female astronauts would only hurt the space program because it would slow down NASA's present space program. Many people stated that as the head of World War II's WASP program and one of the best pilots in the world, Cochran disliked not being involved in any female astronaut training programs.

It was NASA's turn to testify. NASA brought in astronauts John Glenn and Scott Carpenter along with George Low, director of spacecraft and flight missions. Even though Jerrie had twice as many flight hours as Glenn, the astronauts stated that women weren't qualified to be astronauts because they weren't graduates of military jet test piloting programs and didn't possess engineering degrees. Interestingly, Carpenter had not received his aeronautical engineering degree until after he returned from being the second American in space two months earlier. And Glenn had just received his degree from Muskingum College in New Concord, Ohio. Although John Glenn later supported women astronauts, at the time he said the fact that women were not in that field was a fact of our social order.[16]

The hearing ended the next day with no action being taken. The women did not in fact meet the requirements that NASA had set. However, there was a very good reason for this. Women weren't allowed to fly military jets or be pilots for the military in 1962. That wouldn't happen for 15 more years. Jerrie's time flying military planes to South American didn't count. Jean Hixson's stint as a WASP test pilot in World War II didn't count, either.

Jerri Sloan flew B-25s in her business, Air Services. She and her partner (and later, husband) flew the twin-engine bombers that had been used in World War II and Korea. She helped develop Terrain Following Radar (TFR) and "smart" bombs. She tested the equipment by flying at high speeds in the dark over the Gulf of Mexico. But this didn't count as military jet flying, either.

It was a no-win situation for the 13 women who had passed the same testing as the men of the Mercury 7. Manned spaceflight was literally to be just that—for men only. The only female astronaut in the United States for the next 20 years would be Astronaut Barbie.

The next year, the Soviet Union launched the first woman into space, Valentina Tereshkova. Later, when Jerrie met the

Soviet cosmonaut, Valentina told her that everyone had thought Jerrie would be the first woman in space.

Jerrie had, too. She appealed to NASA to restart the program. Interestingly enough, so did Jackie Cochran, who found out that she didn't have any more influence than Jerrie. When Jerrie commented that she was NASA's "most unconsulted consultant," NASA let Jerrie go and replaced her with Cochran.

In America, renewed interest in the subject of women in space emerged after Tereshkova made history. People wanted to know why an American woman hadn't been first in space. Writer, politician, and former ambassador Clare Boothe Luce reported in *Life* magazine that a NASA official said that the idea

Astronaut Barbie

In 1959 the toy company Mattel introduced a doll at the American International Toy Fair in New York. It was known as Barbie and measured just under a foot tall. Unlike baby dolls, Barbie appeared as a miniature-sized young woman with clothes and accessories that could be changed. Barbie was a hit with American children.

Six years after the original Barbie came out, Mattel released Astronaut Barbie. Dressed in a shiny silver space suit, Astronaut Barbie also had a helmet, gloves, and boots. Being an astronaut was one of Barbie's early careers. She later became a dentist, pilot, and basketball player, among many other vocations.

of "an American space woman makes me sick to my stomach." In *Parade* magazine, journalist Jack Anderson said that the only way an American woman would make it into space would be as a guest of a Russian lady cosmonaut.[17]

Luce also named the Mercury 13 publicly for the first time. All thirteen were featured in the magazine. The family of Rhea Hurrle was doubly surprised; they hadn't known about the astronaut testing or that she was such an accomplished pilot. Along with Rhea, the magazine named Myrtle Cagle, Jerrie Cobb, Jan Dietrich, Marion Dietrich, Wally Funk, Sarah Gorelick, Janey Hart, Jean Hixson, Irene Leverton, Jerri Sloan, Gene Nora Stumbough, and B Steadman.

Soon after, NASA recommended 71 military pilots for possible astronaut training. None were women, although three women, including Jerrie Cobb, were among the 271 who had applied. Randy Lovelace, who had started the program, didn't want controversy. After all, he was a respected doctor who had often worked with NASA over the years. He distanced himself from the women and any publicity, believing that diplomacy was the best tactic. NASA had made him head of space medicine after a year. He likely believed that NASA would come around about women astronauts, but he never got to find out. He and his wife died in an airplane crash in 1965.

Although Cochran lived long enough to see the first class of American women astronauts chosen, she did not live long enough to see the first American woman in space. The heart disease that had limited her flying in her later years finally took her life in 1980. Another Mercury 13 member, Marion Dietrich, missed the opportunity to witness the event as well, dying of cancer in 1974. Jean Hixson, a teacher known as the "supersonic schoolmarm," died a year after Sally Ride's historic flight.

Wally Funk, the baby of the group, applied to be an astronaut many times. She, too, was never selected. The first American woman, Sally Ride, didn't go into space until 1983, and she wasn't a pilot. The first female to pilot a spacecraft was Eileen Collins in 1995. Eileen met and talked with the surviving Mercury 13 women. Recognizing that women on space missions owed a lot to these women for paving the way, Eileen invited them to her launch of the STS-63 *Discovery*.

Eight women came, thrilled that a female pilot was finally getting the chance they had been denied so long ago and perhaps a little sad that they weren't flying along with her.

When it was announced that John Glenn would return to space as a payload specialist in 1998, an outcry arose. The mission would study the effects of space on a geriatric astronaut. People who knew about Jerrie began to ask, Why not Jerrie?

Back in the mid-1960s, Jerrie realized that NASA was not going to allow her to join the space program, so she went on a different adventure. She became a missionary pilot, flying supplies to people in the Amazon region of South America. Decades later, when she heard that a petition was being circulated asking that she follow Glenn into space, she returned to American civilization. She gave interviews and again allowed herself to hope, only to hear NASA say no once again. Although she was happy with and fulfilled by her life, she never really forgot about her dream to go into space. She said, "It's what I was born to do. It's my destiny."

Wally Funk went on to other firsts, such as becoming the first female inspector with the Federal Aviation Administration. She has been preparing for a commercial spaceflight and has been to Russia's Star City for cosmonaut training. Wally has bought a ticket to fly on Virgin Galactic's spacecraft, scheduled to launch in December 2013. Dreams may change, but they never die.

LEARN MORE

Almost Astronauts: 13 Women Who Dared to Dream by Tanya Lee Stone (Candlewick Press, 2009).

"Mercury 13—The Women of the Mercury Era." www .mercury13.com.

"Women Who Reach for the Stars." NASA. www.nasa .gov/missions/highlights/f_mercury13.html.

. . . .

PART II

COSMONAUTS

In the late 1950s and early '60s, only two countries had the technology for space travel—the United States and the Soviet Union.

Like many major powers of the 18th century, Russia had been ruled by a monarchy intent on expanding and conquering other lands. However, Russia experienced significant changes in the 20th century. When the Russian Revolution began in 1905, Russia was the largest country in the world. Political reforms resulted in a parliament replacing the monarchy, but problems continued through World War I.

Communists led by Vladimir Lenin overthrew the government in 1917 and instituted a socialist system. Cities were renamed along with the country. Russia became the Union of Soviet Socialist Republics (USSR), more commonly known as the Soviet Union. After Lenin's death, Josef Stalin ruled for 25 years until his death in 1953. Personal freedoms and many lives were lost, but the Soviet Union emerged as a superpower.

This was the political system in which Nikita Khrushchev came to power in 1958. He and the Soviet government believed

strongly that the communist style of government was supe-
rior to the democracy of the United States. An uneasy relationship developed between the two countries after World War II.
Although they had fought on the same side during the war, their
political systems and beliefs were so opposite that each country
worried about the other having too much power, particularly in
regard to nuclear weapons and technology.

Interest in space was strong among Soviet scientists. In 1903, a
rural high school teacher by the name of Konstantin Tsiolkovsy
published the formula for getting rockets into space. Space clubs
sprang up and became a popular pastime for professional scientists, engineers, and serious amateurs. The Moscow Space
Club had more than a thousand members. By the mid-1930s, the
Soviet Ministry of Defense took over the Moscow Space Club.
As technology developed, officials began to see space travel as a
reality. In fact, one Moscow Space Club member was chosen to
design a rocket to go into space.

Sergei Korolev became the chief designer of rockets. The
position brought lots of power. He had a voice in who flew in
his rocket. Korolev wasn't as interested in beating the United
States as he was in seeing his dreams of space travel come true.
Security was important. Only Soviet successes—not Soviet fail-
ures and not American successes—were publicized. He dreamt
that someday people would be living on space colonies. And the
Space Race soon became the contest of the century.

The Soviet Union was first in space when they launched a
satellite named *Sputnik I*. They were also first to launch a living
thing (Laika, a dog), and then a human, Yuri Gagarin. Gagarin,
a test pilot, was launched in the *Vostok 1* capsule on April 12,
1961. He orbited the Earth one time, spending 108 minutes in
space. The first words spoken by a man in space? "I see Earth. It
is so beautiful."[1]

The next natural step in the minds of many in the Soviet Union was to put the first woman in space. Although the US government and NASA said they weren't ready to put a woman in space, the Soviets decided to take up the challenge. Unlike the United States, the Soviet government expected women to work outside of the home, and by the 1950s, many Soviet women were pursuing scientific and technical careers.

The Soviet Union began recruiting women astronauts. Officials asked for single women between the ages of 18 and 30 who had some aviation experience. Parachuting was counted as aviation experience because it required flight. Another plus of parachuting experience was that early cosmonauts had to parachute thousands of feet after reentering the Earth's atmosphere.

Fifty-eight women applied. On January 15, 1962, cosmonaut training director Nikolai Kamanin chose 23 women to undergo additional testing. Like the American women, the Soviet women underwent extensive tests, including both physical examinations and centrifuge testing.

Five women were accepted for cosmonaut training—two from flying clubs, two parachutists, and a rocket propulsion engineer. Although Soviet women had flown as military bomber pilots in World War II, none of the women chosen for the Soviet space program were military pilots.

These women from the western part of the Soviet Union left their homes for the unknown in 1962. A flood of emotions—excitement, fear, uncertainty—accompanied them. But they knew not to show these feelings. Everything they did was being observed and judged. And each wanted to be the first woman in space.

All five women moved to a secret location 40 miles northeast of Moscow, a walled compound filled with people working on the Soviet space program—scientists, engineers, and cosmonauts. It was called Star City.

The women went through an intensive training program. The Soviets wanted to send a woman to space in six months. (Kamanin said that the central objective of this accelerated preparation was to ensure the Americans did not beat the USSR in sending the first woman into space.[2]) The five women took classes in astronomy and aeronautics. Their physical training included swimming and gymnastics. Like the Mercury 13, they also underwent testing for anything they might experience in space.

They were spun in a giant centrifuge to a degree that would make most people severely ill. Could they handle themselves while undergoing violent vibrations or being exposed to extreme forces ten times that of gravity? Placed in a heat chamber kept at 158°F with 30 percent humidity, they remained until their temperatures rose by 4.5°F—to just over 103°F—and their pulses reached 130 beats a minute (normal is 60).

The cosmonauts in training flew in the MiG-15-Spark while the jet made steep climbs and dives. During each dive, they would experience 40-second periods of weightlessness. At the first dive, each cosmonaut had to write her full name and date on a piece of paper. For the next weightlessness test, she had to eat from a tube. In the last phase of weightlessness, she had to pronounce a specific phrase over the radio.

Survival techniques for landing on land and water were part of their training. The women all wore the same size spacesuit for simulated splashdowns in the sea. Made for male cosmonauts, the suits were too big for the women who were just five foot three or five foot four. Additionally, the pressurized space helmets would cause headsets to jerk forward and cover their eyes during an actual splashdown, so they had to practice for this, as well.

For some, the tests and training were easy to deal with compared to the attitudes of the military and the male cosmonauts.

Few supported these efforts to put a woman in space, but after American John Glenn orbited the Earth, the Soviets feared the United States was catching up or even surpassing them in the Space Race.

All five women earned full military and cosmonaut status, but only one would be picked to go into space. US space officials dismissed the Soviet's plans to put a woman in space as more about besting the United States than any scientific interest in women in space. The fact that 19 years would pass before another Soviet woman went into space, and that the second Soviet woman beat America's first women in space by less than a year seemed to support the theory that the Soviet government had little interest in putting women in space.

Another idea batted about was an all-female flight. Chief designer Valentin Glushko felt this would be an important step. More than 2,500 women applied but many were excluded due to their age or ethnicity. Ten women made it past the application process—five physicians, three engineers, a scientist, and a test pilot with an engineering degree. Half of them passed testing and went to Star City to begin training.

Training was made more difficult by the director of Star City, Georgi Beregovoi. Twice, he dropped in on testing and told the women that nothing had been finalized and they had to leave. Both times the women notified Glushko, who would then fix things. When word came that the Americans were going to put their first woman into space, the Soviets dropped plans for an all-female crew and instead focused their energies on launching a second woman into space.

About the same time that the Soviets began working on putting another woman in space, they also began talking about a space station, built from separate modules. The first space station, *Salyut*, was launched into orbit in 1971. It didn't work well, but it was a start. By the late 1970s, the Soviets had come up with a version that had two docking ports. Automatic unmanned space freighters brought supplies.

Each step prepared the Soviets for *Mir*, established in 1986. It was the first permanent space station, staying in orbit for 13 years, until the opening of the International Space Station.

In July 1975, the United States and the Soviet Union had their first joint mission—a Soviet Soyuz capsule docked with a US Apollo module. Construction started on the International Space Station (ISS), which would be used by many countries by the late 20th century. By that time, the Soviet Union had dissolved, and the largest of its republics became the country of Russia once again.

Once the ISS was habitable, spaceflights to the station tended to be made of international crews. In 2011, the United States discontinued its space shuttle program. Currently all flights to the ISS are conducted through the Russian Federal Space Agency.

Only a handful of Soviet women had made spaceflights by 2012, whereas ten times as many American women had become astronauts and gone into space. Just like the United States, Russia is also looking at its next step in space exploration. Exploring Mars is a priority, but a prominent Russian professor of space medicine, Anatoly Grigoryev, says it will be a male-only flight, because women are "too weak" to make the trip. Professor Grigoryev spoke to students at Moscow's International University, stating that women were fragile and delicate creatures, which is why "men should lead the way to distant planets and carry women there in their strong hands."[3]

Grigoryev's comments launched strong responses throughout the space community. Arthur Dula, an American lawyer who specializes in laws governing international space-related activities, stated that such discrimination should make Russia's

Federal Space Agency ineligible for any more funding from the United States.

As Russia advances in space exploration, testing may include a 500-day stint in an isolation chamber. The top six candidates are men. For now, no women are allowed.

VALENTINA TERESHKOVA

. . . .

FIRST IN SPACE

Zhanna Yorkina was a 22-year-old high school teacher who taught foreign languages when a Soviet government official approached her about taking a test. If she passed, she would get to jump from a ship. Zhanna, who enjoyed parachuting and sky-diving, was agreeable. It wasn't until later that she learned that the ship was a spaceship. Although Zhanna was one of the five finalists in this "test," she would not be the one chosen to go into space.

Tatyana Kuznetsova was another of the five finalists, the youngest at only 20 years old. (Fifty years later, she remains

When **Valentina Tereshkova** returned from space, she was honored as a Hero of the Soviet Union and awarded the Order of Lenin and the Gold Star Medal. *Russian International News Agency (RIA Novosti)*

the youngest person ever chosen for a government-sponsored space program.) Tatyana was a secretary, but what she really enjoyed was parachuting, a sport she had taken up in her teens. She loved the feeling of flying in the air. And she was good at it, winning many competitions. Soon after she won the national parachuting championship in 1961, she was recruited for the female cosmonaut program. The skill and courage she showed in parachuting was admired, and she became an early favorite for the spaceflight. But as the intense six-month program began, she experienced problems in the pressure chamber and with the centrifuge. Tatyana would not be the first woman in space, either.

Irina Solovieva was 24 when she became a finalist for cosmonaut training. An engineer, she passed every test given and knew what to do in space. However, flying in space was really only part of the duties that the first woman in space would have to perform. Since Yuri Gagarin had flown into space, he was often called on to speak in public and represent the Soviet Union. The first woman in space would be expected to do the same.

Yet Irina was painfully shy. Although people felt certain that she could handle a spaceflight, they were concerned about what would come afterward. As national heroes, cosmonauts were always in the public eye. When the decision about who would be the first female in space was made, Irina was chosen as the backup. If for some reason the chosen candidate couldn't go into space, Irina would take her place. She also had a chance at a future spaceflight. Her cosmonaut training continued, and Irina was commissioned as an air force cosmonaut. Although she remained with the cosmonaut program through the 1960s, she never got to go into space.

Valentina Ponomaryova was far from shy. As the oldest and most educated of the group of five, she frequently spoke her mind, particularly when it had to do with women's equality. She worked for the Division of Applied Mathematics at the Soviet Academy of Sciences and was recommended for the cosmonaut program by its president, Mstislav Keldysh. Growing up in a family of engineers, Valentina was comfortable in the sciences and performed well in all testing.

When it was time to determine who would be the first woman in space, the decision was made by five men. Keldysh and Sergei Korolev, the chief rocket designer, voted for Valentina. The other three men did not, but she was selected as the second backup and, like Irina, commissioned as a Soviet cosmonaut.

People wondered why Valentina Ponomaryova was not chosen and why she was second backup instead of first. It was suspected that her questions and outspoken behavior were not what Soviet leaders wanted in a national symbol. They wanted someone they were certain would always promote Soviet ideals above her own.

Valentina Ponomaryova later worked as staff head of cosmonautics for the academy. She remained with the cosmonaut program and trained for several flights—the next Vostok, a circumlunar (around the moon) Soyuz flight planned for 1965, and leading an all-female crew on a 10-day mission. All the missions were canceled. Valentina realized that she would never go to space, and in 1969, she retired from the space program.

The last member of the five-woman cosmonaut testing and training group was a 26-year-old textile factory worker. Valentina Tereshkova came from a modest background in the Yaroslavl region. She was the second of three children. Her father died when she was young, and she didn't start school until age 8 or 10 because she was helping her mother. Valentina followed her mother into working at the Krasny Perekop cotton mill at the age of 16.

Valentina discovered parachuting and became quite good at it, making 126 jumps, which brought her to the attention of the Soviet space program. What leader Nikita Khrushchev liked about her was that she represented the best of communist ideals. She was a hard worker, modest, and a leader of the local Komsomol, a youth communist group. Author Stephanie Nolen describes Valentina as "Gagarin in a skirt."[1]

She didn't have as much education as the other young women, but she possessed determination. The night after Yuri Gagarin became the first man in space, Valentina dreamt about being in space. The following day, she volunteered to be a cosmonaut. She worked hard at her studies during the training.

According to fellow cosmonaut Yuri Gagarin, Valentina didn't have it easy. "It was hard for her to master rocket techniques, study spaceship designs and equipment, but she tackled the job stubbornly and devoted much of her own time to study, poring over books and notes in the evening."

And it paid off. She was the clear choice of Soviet leader Khrushchev and of Kamanin, the director of cosmonaut training. Each Valentina had the vote of two men. It fell to Yuri Gagarin, the only man to have actually been to space to make the decision. On May 21, 1963, it was announced that Valentina Tereshkova would be the first woman in space.

Valentina and the two backup cosmonauts continued training for almost another month. They listened to Korolev give inspirational talks about what it meant to be a cosmonaut.

By mid-June, the cosmonauts and everyone affiliated with the space program had traveled to a small town, Tyuratam, east of the Caspian and Aral Seas in Kazakhstan, far from Moscow. Tyuratam was little more than a railway station. It didn't show up on any maps because the Soviet government wanted to keep the isolated, desert-like location a secret. This was the launch site.

On June 14, the three women watched as Valery Bykovsky was launched into orbit in *Vostok 5* at 2:59 PM Moscow time. His launch had been delayed due to various technical problems and high solar activity. The plan was for Valentina to make radio contact with Bykovsky while both cosmonauts were in space.

Two days later, backup Irina and first candidate Valentina suited up in full gear, an orange pressurized spacesuit and helmet. These suits were designed to fit each cosmonaut. Irina's suit tore at the neck. She had to quickly climb into Valentina Ponomaryova's suit, as they were the same size. There wasn't an alternate suit for Valentina Tereshkova, but luckily she had no problems with her suit as she climbed into *Vostok 6*. At 12:30 PM Moscow time, the *Vostok 6* was launched into orbit, and Lieutenant Valentina Tereshkova became the fifth cosmonaut in space.

Minutes after launching, Valentina was heard speaking with Bykovsky. "It is I, Sea Gull." Cosmonauts had code names, and hers was Sea Gull. Bykovsky's was Falcon. The two ships came within three miles of each other. "I see the horizon. A light blue, a beautiful band. This is the Earth. How beautiful it is! All goes well."[2]

Within ninety minutes, Soviet and European television audiences watched a live telecast of Valentina in her capsule. She was smiling as her logbook and pencil floated past her. The world watched history being made. Not only was the first woman in space, but two space capsules were in orbit at the same time. Bykovsky was also setting a record for time in space.

In reality, the cosmonauts were experiencing difficulties. The *Vostok 5*, Bykovsky's spacecraft, was in a lower orbit than planned. That and the solar activity caused high temperatures in the capsule, and he had to return early.

Valentina spent three days in space, making 48 orbits around the Earth. Not only was she the first woman in space, but her time in space exceeded the time spent by all of the US astronauts combined.

Inside the capsule, things were going well. But the Soviet capsules were very small. Valentina's helmet, fitted with electrodes, was also uncomfortable. Space-induced nausea is common in spaceflight, and Valentina wasn't the first to have it. Although Valentina made radio contact with Bykovsky and chatted on television with Khrushchev, she didn't do all that was required of her. She did some filming but didn't make her log entries until after landing. She also refused to do medical tests on the first female body in space.

Upon reentry on June 19, the *Vostok 6* was delayed because of problems that were not made public at the time. When Valentina was ejected from the ship, she parachuted several hundred miles northeast of the city of Karaganda. A group of villagers surrounded her and took her to her ship.

The world applauded Valentina Tereshkova. She was honored as a Hero of the Soviet Union and awarded the Order of Lenin and the Gold Star Medal. She became a symbol of equality and a positive symbol for the Soviet Union. At the United Nations, she received a standing ovation and the World Peace Council Joliot-Curie Gold Medal. She was much in demand as a spokesperson for the Soviet Union.

Closer to home, members of the Soviet space agency were furious with her performance. Star City physicians reported that she demonstrated a weak mental and physical performance. One leading doctor, Vasily Mishin, suggested that she had experienced a breakdown.

Valentina quietly insisted that was not the case; she said something had been wrong with the flight. She was ignored, and her reputation at Star City suffered. When explaining why she didn't speak up, Valentina said, "We don't think of fear, we only think of responsibility."[3]

Almost five months later, Valentina married another cosmonaut, Andrian Nikolayev, who had been the third cosmonaut in space. The marriage of the two cosmonauts received much interest, as did their daughter, Elena, the first child of parents who had both been exposed to space. Elena suffered no effects from her parents' travels.

Valentina continued to work at Star City until 1997, although the cosmonaut group was disbanded in 1969. After retiring from Star City, Valentina held various government offices, such as people's deputy and deputy to the Supreme Soviet, and she served on committees. Today, she makes occasional public appearances and gives interviews supporting women astronauts.

After the Soviet Union broke up, more details about Valentina's flight were brought to light. She had been correct when she stated that something was wrong. She had noticed that her ship was pointed in the wrong direction. If she had fired her retrorockets when originally instructed to, she would have been pushed farther out into space without a way to return. When Ground Control realized she was correct, they sent new commands to Valentina to get her back home. Instead of admitting a problem, the Soviet space agency blamed Valentina. As a good citizen, she never tried to publicly contradict her country.

LEARN MORE

Almost Heaven: The Story of Women in Space by Bettyann Holtzmann Kevles (Basic Books, 2006).

NASA. www.nasa.gov/mission_pages/station/multimedia /gallery/jsc2010e193858.html.

"Valentina Tereshkova." NASA. http://starchild.gsfc.nasa .gov/docs/StarChild/whos_who_level2/tereshkova .html.

SVETLANA SAVITSKAYA

. . . .

NO APRON FOR HER

Svetlana Savitskaya looked down on Earth from space to see the cities sparkling like stars. After 19 years of promised and canceled flights, the Soviet Union had just launched the second woman into space from the Soviet space center in Baikonur. It was 1982, and research cosmonaut Svetlana Savitskaya was taking an eight-day journey into space along with two male cosmonauts aboard the *Soyuz* T-7. Although she was a pilot, her role on this spaceflight was as a researcher. The three cosmonauts were journeying to a Soviet space station, the *Salyut 7*, where they would rendezvous with two other cosmonauts who had been at the station for six months.

The second woman in space, **Svetlana Savitskaya**, was the first to take a space walk. *RIA Novosti/Science Photo Library*

As the Soyuz spacecraft docked with the Salyut space station, the three cosmonauts made their way on board. Anatoly Berezovoy and Valentin Lebedev welcomed them. Flight engineer Lebedev greeted Svetlana and said, "We've got an apron ready for you, Sveta. It's as if you've come home. Of course, we have a kitchen for you; that'll be where you work."[1]

Svetlana was stunned. She had set world records with supersonic aircraft, including a speed record of 2,683 kph in a MiG-21. A former all-around world aerobatics champion, she was qualified to pilot 20 types of aircraft. Now she had finally taken the ultimate flight into space only to have her fellow cosmonauts joking about her cooking for them?

She knew that her future and the future of other Soviet women in space travel depended upon her ability to get along with others. Gritting her teeth, she responded, "And I thought you would be the one to fix us something to eat." Her fellow cosmonauts laughed and later said that she was "as good as a man," which they considered quite a compliment.

Svetlana was used to proving herself. She was the daughter of Veveniy Savitsky, the deputy commander of the Soviet Air Defense and a World War II pilot, so people liked to say that her father's position opened doors for her. Yet Svetlana worked harder than everyone else to prove she could succeed on her own. No one could say she wasn't qualified for flight.

Born in Moscow, Svetlana knew she wanted to be a pilot at age 16. Although she applied to local flight schools, she was turned down due to her age—so she took up parachute training. She did this secretly without her parents' knowledge, until the day her father found her parachute knife in her school bag. Svetlana's father must have seen the determination in his daughter's eyes. By the time she turned 17, she had made 450 parachute jumps and, with her father's help, at the age of 17, she made a stratospheric (the second layer of atmosphere) sky dive from 14,252 meters.

Soon after turning 18, Svetlana began flight training at Moscow Aviation Institute. She continued parachuting and competed with the Soviet National Aerobatics Team in England in 1970. Not only was she the World Champion, but the British media nicknamed her "Miss Sensation."

After graduating from the Moscow Aviation Institute with an engineering degree, she worked as a flight trainer for the USSR Voluntary Society for the Promotion of the Army, Air Force, and Navy. She pushed on to be a test pilot and was finally accepted for training. She began testing for the Yakovlev Design Bureau.

When the Soviet Union heard that the United States was planning to launch the country's first female into space aboard the space shuttle, the Soviet space agency committed to putting another Soviet woman into space. That woman was Svetlana. She was one of three women recruited and trained for an all-female flight. The others were Irina Pronina and Natalya Kuleshova.

After the conclusion of a successful mission as the 53rd cosmonaut sent into space, Svetlana continued training. She planned to return to space. She also tried to ignore the condescending remarks by TASS, the government news agency, about her being of the fair sex. A daily newspaper, *Izvestia*, decided her biography needed to be balanced with traditionally feminine attributes, so they wrote, "She is charming and soft, a hospitable hostess and likes to make patterns and sew her own clothes when she has time to spare."[2]

Almost two years after her first flight, Svetlana took off again on July 17, 1984, this time as a flight engineer on the *Soyuz* T-12 for an 11-day mission. Svetlana again traveled to the space station *Salyut 7*. This trip provided her with two opportunities—not only was she the first woman to make two trips into space, 34-year-old Svetlana would be the first woman to conduct an extravehicular activity (EVA), better known as a space walk.

Svetlana's second mission allowed the Soviet Union to best the United States yet again. NASA already had a planned spaceflight for October 1984 in which an American woman, Kathryn D. Sullivan, would take a space walk, and another woman, Sally Ride, would be making her second flight.

Svetlana spent 3 hours and 58 minutes on the space walk. She and cosmonaut Vladimir Dzhanibekov took turns conducting welding and soldering experiments. When one welded, the other filmed. They tested a 66-pound, general purpose, hand-operated tool. Although the tool was weightless in space, it was still difficult to operate, requiring the cosmonauts to expend a lot of energy with each movement.

The Soviet press and government seemed conflicted about the presence of women in space, however. Reports of women in science and other important professions occurred frequently, but there was also much discussion about the differences. The primary role of women as wives and mothers was never far from the discussion of the achievements of Soviet women.

In a press conference after the flight, Svetlana couldn't hide her irritation at remarks made about women bringing a pleasant atmosphere to a space station. She had just walked in space! She told reporters, "We do not go into space to improve the mood of the crew. Women go into space because they measure up to the job. They can do it."[3]

Twice honored with the Hero of the Soviet Union award, Svetlana worked as a flight engineer. She remained on the active cosmonaut list while working first as a civilian engineer and later as deputy to the chief designer at NPO Energia, the rocket design company that worked with the Soviet space program. There were plans for her to command an all-female crew on International Women's Day on April 3, 1986, but it was canceled due to a lack of Soyuz spacecraft.

Svetlana never flew in space again. She retired as a major from the cosmonaut program in 1993, having spent 19.71 days in space. She went on to work in government as a member of the Russian legislature and deputy chair of the Committee on Defense.

LEARN MORE

Almost Heaven: The Story of Women in Space by Bettyann Holtzmann Kevles (Basic Books, 2006).

"Facts About Spacesuits and Spacewalking." NASA. www .nasa.gov/audience/foreducators/spacesuits/facts/facts -index.html.

"Svetlana Savitskaya." International Space Hall of Fame. www.nmspacemuseum.org/halloffame/detail.php ?id=89.

Women Astronauts by Laura S. Woodmansee (Collector's Guide Publishing, 2002).

Women in Space: Reaching the Last Frontier by Carole S. Briggs (Lerner Books, 1998).

ELENA KONDAKOVA

....

LONG DURATION IN SPACE

After the country sent two women into space on three different spaceflights, one might assume that gender barriers in space were a thing of the past for the Soviet Union. But that wasn't the case. Without specific motivation, such as winning against the United States, it seemed the Soviet men in charge of the programs did not see any justification to put a woman into space.

Starting in the 1980s, the Soviet Union was facing economic and political upheaval. Communist rule was failing. More than

---

(Left to right) Mission specialists Jean-François Clervoy of the European Space Agency, **Elena V. Kondakova** of the Russian Space Agency, and Edward Tsang Lu of NASA outside of the SPACEHAB Double Module, which carried more than 6,000 pounds of scientific experiments to the Russian Space Station *Mir. Kennedy Space Center*

a third of the national budget was going to the military, leaving people hungry and without jobs. Countries that had been annexed by the Soviet Union wanted more independence. They received that in 1991 when the Soviet Union dissolved.

During the political upheaval of the uncertain 1990s, the third female Russian cosmonaut was in training. Born in the Moscow region in a town called Mytishchi in 1957, Elena Kondakova had graduated from Moscow Bauman High Technical College in 1980 and began working for RSC Energia, the company that was making many of the rockets used in Russian spaceflights. Elena's job involved science experiments and research work. Her exceptional work skills and abilities were noticed, and RSC Energia's main design bureau recommended her as a cosmonaut.

Elena began general space training at the Gagarin Cosmonaut Training Center. She completed the course in March 1990, and her status was changed to "test cosmonaut." The chance she had been waiting for came in 1994, when she began six months of training for the Euromir 94 spaceflight, also known as the 17th main mission. Elena trained with another cosmonaut, German/ESA astronaut Ulf Merbold, for a long stay at the *Mir* Space Station.

Elena launched with the crew on October 4, 1994, the first female to take part in a long-duration flight. As flight engineer, she assisted the *Soyuz* TM-17 in reaching the *Mir* Space Station, where she spent five months.

By this time, Soviet cosmonauts flew and shared missions with astronauts from other countries. In addition to the month with Merbold, Elena worked with NASA astronaut Norman Thagard for five days. She returned to Earth from a successful mission on March 22, 1995, after 169 days in space.

Slightly more than two years after her first flight, Elena returned to the *Mir* Space Station on a shorter flight. This time,

Mir Space Station

The *Mir* Space Station wasn't the first or only space station to orbit Earth, but it was the longest-lasting one, withstanding 15 years and 86,000 orbits. Like the outposts of the American West, *Mir* became a place for astronauts throughout the world to visit. And it taught the world how to build an international space station.

The Russian word *mir* means "world" or "village." Traveling 250 miles above Earth, *Mir* was an odd-looking structure with modules added here and there, including *Kvant I*, *Kvant II*, *Kristall*, and a docking module. Like people trying to find pictures in the clouds, those lucky enough to see *Mir* did the same when looking at the space station. It was described as a dragonfly, a hedgehog, and a Tinkertoy.

Mir set every record in long-duration spaceflight. Physician Valeri Polyakov set a record for the longest single time spent in space, living on *Mir* for 437 days, 17 hours, and 38 minutes. Polyakov was one of 125 cosmonauts and astronauts to visit the space station, which hosted 17 space expeditions.

Mir lasted longer than anyone thought it would, but it eventually began sinking in its orbit around the time that construction on the International Space Station began. It was agreed that *Mir* should be allowed to die a natural death, which it did on March 23, 2001, when it broke up while reentering the atmosphere, landing in the southern Pacific Ocean about 1,800 miles east of New Zealand.

she flew on NASA's *Atlantis* as a mission specialist. Mission STS-84 returned May 24, 1997. This mission lasted 9 days, 5 hours, and 20 minutes. Once Elena completed her second flight, she could say that she had logged more than 178 days in space.

Elena was honored as a Hero of Russia for her spaceflights. She married another cosmonaut, Valery Ryumin, with whom she has one child.

Although there was talk of Elena returning to space, her interests changed to politics. In 1999, she began serving in the State Duma, Russia's parliament, which is similar to the US House of Representatives.

LEARN MORE

Almost Heaven: The Story of Women in Space by Bettyann Holtzmann Kevles (Basic Books, 2006).

"Elena V. Kondakova: Russian Cosmonaut." NASA. www .jsc.nasa.gov/Bios/htmlbios/kondakov.html.

"Elena V. Kondakova." NASA. http://spaceflight.nasa .gov/history/shuttle-mir/people/p-c-kondakova.htm.

Women Astronauts by Laura S. Woodmansee (Collector's Guide Publishing, 2002).

YELENA SEROVA

· · · · · · · · · · · · · · · ·

READY AND WAITING

In the 15 years since Elena Kondakova's voyage to the *Mir* Space Station in 1997, not a single female cosmonaut has gone on a spaceflight. After Kondakova, Nadezhda Kuzhelnaya was the only woman cosmonaut in the Russian Space Program. Although she was part of the program for 10 years and viewed as very capable, she was never offered a spaceflight.

According to a Russian Federal Space Agency representative, Vitaly Davydov, the program just hasn't received many applications from women. As of late 2012, there is only one female cosmonaut. She is Yelena Serova. Born April 22, 1976, Yelena is part of the next generation of astronauts. She wasn't even born

---

In 2014, **Yelena Serova** will be the first female cosmonaut in space in 17 years when she travels to the International Space Station. *www.spacefacts.de*

Star City

....

Officially, it's the Yuri Gagarin Cosmonaut Training Center, but to the thousands who have trained there and the millions who have read about it, it is Star City. When the Soviet Union began making plans to send a man into space, space industry leaders knew they needed a special cosmonaut training facility.

Testing and training were performed at temporary locations until a permanent one was found near the Chkalovskaya train station. It was close enough to be accessible to government leaders—only 40 kilometers from Moscow—but it was far enough to be private.

The Cosmonaut Training Center opened its doors in 1960. Security was tight, and its location was to be kept a secret. Not only was it a training facility, but it also had residences that housed cosmonauts, scientists, and space personnel and their families. When astronauts from other countries came to train, new cottages housed them during their visits.

Originally operated by the Russian Air Force, Star City is now under the control of Roscosmos, the Russian Space Agency. According to the media, there are more than 2,000 people working at Star City, and 30 percent of those jobs are critical to the space agency.

Star City contains full-size mock-ups of spacecraft, a hydro-laboratory large enough for a 20-ton space module, special aircraft that simulate weightlessness, two centrifuges, and a planetarium with the capacity to show 9,000 stars.

when Valentina Tereshkova made her historic flight. Many people have high hopes that Yelena can achieve what so few Russian women have been able to—flying into space.

Yelena remembers one of her earliest teachers talking about space, and ever since then Yelena has yearned to be closer to the stars. She graduated from Moscow Aviation Institute. Selected for the Russian space program in 2006, Yelena completed basic training at Star City in 2009 and is currently a test cosmonaut.

Yelena sees the cosmonaut as a combination of scientist and athlete, and she enjoys the challenges of training. When three times her weight is pushing down on her in g-force training, she has to concentrate and remember to breathe. Yelena has passed survival tests at sea, in forests, and in deserts. In late 2011, Russian Space Agency chief Vladimir Popovkin announced that Yelena would fly to the International Space Station.

In November 2012, the Russian Space Agency said it was working through a selection process that would include a number of female cosmonaut candidates, but no names have been mentioned since then, so it remains to be seen how many women will go to space.

Yelena is scheduled to fly to the International Space Station as a flight engineer for Expedition 41/42. Part of her training has occurred at the simulation and training facility at Johnson Space Center. The plan is for Yelena to spend up to six months performing biophysics and medical experiments. Her husband and daughter support her dreams, particularly her husband, cosmonaut Mark Serov. Who knows? Perhaps she will set a new record for women in space.

A History of Russian Spaceflight

The Space Age began when the Soviet Union launched the world's first artificial satellite, *Sputnik I*, in 1957. Scientists had been working on the project since 1946. The next step was launching a living thing, a dog named Laika, in *Sputnik II* less than a month later. Laika was a stray on the Moscow streets when she was picked for a spaceflight. Although *Sputnik* was outfitted with an oxygen generator, a carbon dioxide–absorbing device, and a fan, the mixed-breed dog was not expected to live through the flight. The Soviets stated that she lived up to a week before the sensors failed.

In 2002, more information was released. Laika died within five to seven hours of launch from stress and overheating. *Sputnik II* orbited the earth 2,570 times before it burned up in the atmosphere five months later. Laika's sacrifice made the following highlights possible in Soviet and Russian space exploration:

January 2, 1959: The Soviet Union launches *Luna 1*. Although it misses its target of the moon, it is the first artificial object to leave Earth's orbit.

September 12, 1959: *Luna 2* is launched and crashes into the moon on purpose.

October 24, 1960: A Mars probe, the *R-16 ICBM*, explodes at the Baikonur Cosmodrome during prelaunch, killing 126 people.

(continued on the next page)

February 12, 1961: A Venus probe, *Venera*, is launched to Venus but stops working after a week.

April 12, 1961: Yuri Gagarin becomes the first man in space with a 108-minute flight on *Vostok 1*.

June 16, 1963: Valentina Tereshkova becomes the first woman to fly into space.

October 12, 1964: *Voskhod 1*, a modified Vostok orbiter with a three-person crew, is launched.

March 18, 1965: Soviet cosmonaut Alexei Leonov becomes the first person in the world to make a spacewalk.

February 3, 1966: Unmanned Soviet spacecraft *Luna 9* lands on the moon.

March 1, 1966: The *Venera 3* probe lands on the planet Venus, but the communications system fails.

April 3, 1966: The *Luna 10* space probe becomes the first spacecraft to orbit the moon.

April 23, 1967: *Soyuz 1* launches, but there are problems. The parachute doesn't open upon return to Earth, killing Soviet cosmonaut Vladimir Komarov.

January 16, 1969: *Soyuz 4* and *Soyuz 5* dock and make the first in-orbit crew transfer.

April 19, 1971: The first space station, *Salyut 1*, is launched.

June 6, 1971: *Soyuz 11* successfully docks with *Salyut 1*, but the cosmonauts die during reentry from a pressure leak.

July 17, 1975: The first docking of a Soviet spacecraft, *Soyuz 19*, and a US spacecraft, *Apollo 18*, takes place.

September 29, 1977: *Salyut 6* is the first space station equipped with docking stations on either end, which allow for two vehicles to dock at once.

February 20, 1986: The Soviet Union launches the *Mir* Space Station.

March 13, 1986: *Mir* is powered up by the crew of *Soyuz T-15*.

November 15, 1988: The Soviet Union launches the *Buran* space shuttle.

November 20, 1998: The first part of the International Space Station, the Russian module *Zarya*, is launched.

LEARN MORE

Yelena Serova photo. NASA. http://spaceflight.nasa.gov /gallery/images/station/crew-41/html/jsc2012e237552 .html.

PART III

....

AMERICAN WOMEN JOIN THE SPACE RACE

On an early February day in 1995, soon after midnight, a crowd gathered to watch the latest launch of the space shuttle *Discovery*. The pilot of Mission STS-63 had invited special guests to the launch. They included Myrtle Cagle, Jerrie Cobb, Wally Funk, Gene Nora (Stumbough) Jessen, Sarah (Gorelick) Rutley, B Steadman, and Jerri (Sloan) Truhill—seven members of the Mercury 13. These women had once shared a dream of flying in space, but were denied by their country. Instead, a female Soviet cosmonaut with far less flight experience took the honors of being the first woman in space.

Several American women had flown in space, but astronaut Eileen Collins was special to the Mercury 13. Like them, she was a pilot. And on that day, she would be the first woman in the world to pilot a spacecraft into space. Although it had been too long in coming, the women of the Mercury 13 were still amazed that the day had finally arrived.

When the military began accepting women for pilot training in the 1970s, NASA opened up the astronaut corps. It was a new era in spaceflight. The Apollo and Gemini capsules were replaced by the space shuttle, NASA's program of repurposing spacecraft to explore space. Its official name was the Space Transportation System (STS), and it contained the orbiter, which is what we think of when we think of a space shuttle. But the STS was actually a stack of parts with three space shuttle main engines, twin solid rocket boosters, and a giant external fuel tank. By the time the shuttle reached orbit, all the parts except the orbiter would be jettisoned as they would no longer be needed.

Mercury 13 astronauts (from left to right) Gene Nora (Stumbough) Jessen, Wally Funk, Jerrie Cobb, Jerri (Sloan) Truhill, Sarah (Gorelick) Rutley, Myrtle Cagle, and Bernice Steadman prepare to witness the liftoff of STS-63, piloted by Eileen Collins. *NASA*

Astronauts no longer had to be pilots unless they were piloting or commanding the shuttle. Now there were other opportunities for scientists as mission specialists and payload specialists— scientists who could contribute to the exploration of space. In 1977, NASA began advertising for this kind of astronaut. This time, women and minorities were encouraged to apply.

After six months of advertising, only 93 women had sent in applications. Nichelle Nichols, a television icon who starred on *Star Trek*, lent her support to the recruitment effort, and numbers increased. In the summer of 1977, NASA announced that it had 208 finalists for its next class of astronauts. Twenty-one were women.

The astronaut class of 1978 included six women. They ranged in age from 26 to 39. All were intelligent, goal-driven women, including two engineers, two physicians, and two scientists. The first six American female astronauts selected by NASA were Anna Fisher, Shannon Lucid, Judith Resnik, Sally Ride, Margaret Rhea Seddon, and Kathryn Sullivan. After they completed their training in August 1979, they worked in various specialties at Johnson Space Center in Houston—and they waited for their names to be called up.

Sally Ride was the first to receive a mission, followed by Judith Resnick. Both Anna Fisher and her astronaut husband, William, received assignments in late 1983, although not together. Her flight was scheduled for 1984, three months before his. Both Anna Fisher and Kathryn Sullivan had their first flights in 1984. Margaret Rhea Seddon's first of three flights into space took place a year later, as did the first of Shannon Lucid's many flights.

With the addition of women in space came jokes about women needed for cleanup duty. The women learned to take the gibes in stride and keep the smiles on their faces. Kathryn Sullivan came up with the best line she could: *Only happy to do*

Help to the Final Frontier
from *Star Trek*

• •

NASA had help from the television series *Star Trek* in the recruitment of women. Public interest in space travel had done wonders for the science fiction television show starring William Shatner and Leonard Nimoy—that is, after creator Gene Roddenberry rewrote the first script. Originally, he envisioned a female captain. But sponsors said no way, and Roddenberry turned the captain into a man.

In the 1970s, NASA attended a *Star Trek* convention, hoping to recruit women and minorities. In the audience was actress Nichelle Nichols, better known as Lieutenant Uhura on the TV series. As she gazed at a podium filled with white men, Nichols challenged them. They in turn recruited her to tackle the task of encouraging women and minorities to apply to be astronauts. She visited high schools and colleges. She talked to young minority scientists and professionals. And she recruited Guion Bluford Jr., the first African American in space.

Another one of her recruits was the brilliant Mae Jemison. Mae later became the first real astronaut on *Star Trek* when she did a cameo in *Star Trek: The Next Generation*.

For Nichols's efforts in recruiting women and minorities for the space program, she was presented with the NASA Distinguished Public Service Award in 1984 by astronaut Judith Resnik.

America's first class of females astronauts included (from left to right) Sally Ride, Judith Resnik, Anna Fisher, Kathryn Sullivan, and Margaret Rhea Seddon. *NASA*

windows, but only from the outside. In the early years of women in the space program, women only accounted for about 6 percent of the total group. Today, one out of every five astronauts is a woman. Compare that to one out of every seven police officers and one out of every 20 pilots.

In 1994, the United States and Russia began plans for the International Space Station. The United States would provide $400 million so that *Mir* could be extended and seven US astronauts could experience long-duration missions on the Russian space station. This meant training in Star City in Russia. Two of the first were Norman Thagard, who was chosen as the first American to go to *Mir*, and his backup, Bonnie Dunbar.

They arrived at Star City in 1994, and Bonnie was amazed at the attitudes she was subjected to because of her gender. Russian men saw nothing wrong with putting their arms around her and telling her she was beautiful. She wasn't allowed to use the cosmonaut gym because there was no women's dressing room.

She felt very alone. Although she didn't get to go to *Mir*, she was part of the shuttle crew that picked up Norman Thagard at the end of his stay at *Mir* and returned him to Earth.

By 2012, 43 American women—astronauts—had been to space. There have been 55 women astronauts in the world, and 78 percent of those are American. Although they were late to the Space Race, they have grown like no other country's astronauts. American women have served as payload specialists, mission specialists, flight engineers, pilots, and commanders of both space shuttles and space stations. They have held every astronaut postition.

One of these astronauts, Mary Cleave, has traveled nearly four million miles in space. When she attended college at Colorado State University in 1965, she started as a preveterinary student, but she wasn't accepted to veterinary schools. Only two women were accepted, so she switched to botany. She attended graduate school at Utah State University, and she later earned her doctorate in civil and environmental engineering.

One day, Mary noticed a poster in the post office. NASA, billing itself as an affirmative action employer, was looking for astronauts. Mary applied and was accepted in 1980. Working for NASA for 27 years, she was thrilled to go on two spaceflights.

Mary travels and speaks of her experiences today. She promotes more girls joining science, technology, engineering, and mathematics (STEM) programs. Mary said she got used to being the only girl in the room when she was in school, and it wasn't so bad. "That's why I say: 'Don't be afraid.' . . . [Men] won't bite you. And if they do, bite back."[1]

Another astronaut, Dorothy Metcalf-Lindenburger, says, "It isn't like space exploration in the '50s and '60s, which was a very traditional America. As we've grown into the 21st century, we are seeing that there are no set roles. Women need to learn about

STEM

Have you heard of STEM programs? STEM stands for science, technology, engineering, and math. These subjects teach future astronauts what they need to know to go into space. For example, almost all parts of spaceflight require the understanding of math. Releasing a satellite requires calculations using angles.

People once believed that boys did better in subjects like math and sciences. Later, it was shown that girls did just as well as boys in these subjects until middle school or junior high school. What happens then? According to teachers, many girls at this age often decide that science and math are no longer cool. Girls also face stereotypes that tell them they can't be as good at science and math as boys. In 1966, only about 50,000 women earned engineering or science degrees as opposed to more than 184,000 men.

Forty-two years later, the number of graduates who have earned STEM degrees are in the millions. The growth for women has been higher than men (37 percent as opposed to 24 percent). Women only earn about 40 percent of the STEM degrees awarded in the United States. Hopefully that number will continue to rise.

Girls can do math and science just as well as boys—sometimes better.

technology because [the field] wasn't as female-dominated then and now there are opportunities for both men and women."[2]

American women are very much a part of space travel. They have been a part of both the triumphs and the tragedies. When American women first went into space, they were surrounded by lots of media attention, much more so than the male astronauts they were flying with. Many women astronauts found this attention uncomfortable. It singled them out as something special or something different, which is another way of not really being equal.

Today, when women make spaceflights, their names are mentioned alongside their fellow male astronauts, but not as women astronauts—just as astronauts. This is the biggest indicator that women have been accepted in space programs.

Astronauts know that going into space is not without risks. Each astronaut who goes into space is risking her life, yet it is something each one is driven to do. They are all, without a doubt, women of courage.

Bathrooms in Space

One of the most common questions people have about spaceflight is how you go to the bathroom in space. Remember that the limited gravity means that things don't necessarily go down.

In the early days, for shorter flights, astronauts were hooked up to bags that would collect urine and feces. Longer flights meant that a zero-gravity toilet had to be designed. Urine went into special funnels. Instead of water flushing the toilet, air was forced into it to push waste to a collection area. The first of these toilets had a 14-day limit on how much they could hold. For Mission STS-54, a new kind of toilet was introduced. A plastic bag is put in the toilet before use; after use, the bag is sealed, and a special kind of plunger-level forces the bag into a cylinder.

SALLY RIDE

....

FIRST AMERICAN WOMAN IN SPACE

On June 18, 1983, the space shuttle *Challenger* blasted off from Kennedy Space Center at 7:33 in the morning. This *Challenger* mission, STS-7, was the seventh space shuttle flight and the second flight for the *Challenger*.

After eight and a half minutes, the five astronauts heard the shuttle's engines cut off. They all knew what that meant. They were officially in orbit. One astronaut undid the straps on her seat and floated over to look out the window. Her first view of the planet left her speechless: coral reefs off Australia, a dust storm in northern Africa, and a huge storm churning in the ocean. She said to herself, *Spectacular!*

Sally Ride, the first US woman in space, looks out from the flight deck. *NASA*

Suddenly, Mission Control summoned the group. The space-craft commander, Captain Robert L. Crippen, gave a report. Afterward, Mission Control asked astronaut Sally Ride, the first American woman in space, about the trip. She grinned and answered that it was definitely an E-ticket ride.[1] As anyone who had ever visited Disneyland or Walt Disney World at the time knew, E tickets were reserved for the most popular and exciting rides in the amusement parks.

The 32-year-old mission specialist was also the youngest American in space so far, but she had a very special job. The mission would be launching two communications satellites in addition to conducting 10 experiments. Much of the focus was on the historic event of an American woman being sent to space, but Dr. Sally Ride, a physicist, had work to do.

One very important job was testing the shuttle's huge 50-foot robotic arm, which would be used to deploy and retrieve a satellite. Operating the robotic arm was like operating a very difficult video game. Although most video games require the use of both hands, they only require one controller. Sally had to use two hand controllers to move the arm where she wanted it to go. With one, she moved the arm up and down and side to side. The other controller allowed her to rotate the arm. Intent on her task, she captured the satellite. Like Jerrie Cobb, Sally knew the chance for other women to go to space depended on whether she did a good job.

One the third day of the mission, the crew discovered an impact crater had hit the shuttle. Some foreign object, perhaps a very small micrometeorite, had caused a dent 3/16 of an inch wide and 1/16 of an inch deep. Fortunately, the dent caused no problems for the space shuttle. A bigger deal was when the shuttle toilet malfunctioned on day five.

Sleeping in Space

The exhilaration of being in space, something she had trained five years for, left the idea of sleep low on her list of things to do, but Sally knew she needed sleep to perform well. The question was how to do that. Some shuttles had sleeping compartments, but they looked like coffins. For the first two nights, Sally tried sleeping in the shuttle's blue sleeping bags, which were attached at the head and foot to the mid-deck so she wouldn't float into something. On the third night, she detached her sleeping bag and floated. On night four, she traded the shuttle bag for a white Apollo sleeping bag that she attached to a handrail in the air lock.

After 6 days, 2 hours, 23 minutes, and 59 seconds, the *Challenger* landed at Edwards Air Force Base in California. Sally knew she would have to talk to the media again. That wasn't one of her favorite things to do, and NASA flight director Chris Kraft had sat her down before the flight to talk to her about it. Yet in her excitement, she let much of what he said fly past her. Later she recalled some ridiculous preflight questions she'd heard. One person asked whether she was going to cry in space. Her response was, "Why doesn't Rick [the pilot] get asked that question?"[2] Someone else asked her how much she was getting paid, and her answer was a very honest one: "I mean, who cares? I'd pay them."[3]

The *Challenger* crew arrived at the press conference. They showed movies of their voyage and the capture of a science satellite with the robotic arm. But what the media wanted to know was how the first woman in space had performed. Captain Crippen reported that there were no problems, and that he would gladly fly with Dr. Ride again. A physician on the crew, Dr. Norman E. Thagard, reported no differences in the way Dr. Ride adapted to zero gravity compared to the men.

Sally Ride wrote in her autobiography, "The thing that I'll remember most about the flight is that it was fun. In fact, I'm sure it was the most fun I'll ever have in my life."[4]

Sally and pilot Rick Hauck were asked to go on a goodwill tour of Europe. They visited eight countries, met royalty and other important people, gave interviews, and made presentations. When they attended the International Astronautical Federation conference in Budapest, Hungary, Sally was invited to a private meeting with cosmonaut Svetlana Savitskaya, the second woman in space. Although it had been suggested that Sally and Rick keep their distance from the cosmonauts, Sally couldn't ignore this opportunity. No report of the meeting was ever made. Chances are that Svetlana Savitskaya wasn't supposed to spend time with Sally Ride, either. The Cold War may have thawed, but there continued to be a lack of trust between the two countries.

Becoming an astronaut hadn't crossed young Sally's mind when she watched astronauts splashing down on television along with thousands of children across the country. "I can still remember teachers wheeling those big old black-and-white television sets into the classroom, so that we could watch some of the early space launches and splashdowns."[5]

Born in Los Angeles in 1951, Sally had an enjoyable childhood growing up in Encino. A good student, she was quiet in class and dreaded being called on, even when she knew the answer.

She loved being outside and being active, so she gravitated to sports. As a teenager, she ranked 18th in the nation for tennis in her age group. A tennis scholarship got her admitted to a private girls' school, Westlake High School, in Los Angeles. She was nationally ranked and tennis legend Billie Jean King suggested that Sally turn professional, but when a high school physiology teacher awakened Sally's love of the scientific method, she traded tennis for academics.

When it was time for college, she moved to Pennsylvania to attended Swarthmore College. After three semesters, she transferred to Stanford University in her beloved California. She received bachelor's degrees in both physics and English. In graduate school, she decided to pursue a master's in physics. Focusing her studies on X-ray astronomy and free-electron lasers, she wanted to know how electrons would act in the magnetic fields of space.

Sally continued with physics in Stanford's PhD program because she thought she would like to teach the subject someday. One day, she opened the student newspaper and saw on page three an advertisement that said NASA was looking for new astronauts. Finally, women were encouraged to apply. Astronaut candidates didn't need to be pilots, either; NASA was also looking for scientists. "The moment I saw that ad, I knew that's what I wanted to do," she said.[6]

Sally applied to NASA and went on to finish her PhD, receiving her degree in 1978. In the late 1970s, women held only about 4 percent of all earned physics degrees. Then Sally competed against 8,370 others for the chance to be an astronaut. In January 1978, NASA announced the next astronaut group of 35 people, including six women. Sally was one of the six.

Sally began the astronaut training program, which included gravity training, radio communication and navigation, water survival, and parachute jumping. She worked as the communications officer for the second and third space shuttle missions, talking to the astronauts from Mission Control. She found fly-ing T-38 jets so interesting that she earned her pilot's license. After a year of training, she became eligible for a spaceflight.

Sally was chosen to go into space first because of her exper-tise with the robotic arm. She would be a mission specialist on Mission STS-7 aboard the shuttle *Challenger* in 1983. Training and preparing for her spaceflight took up much of her days, but she took time to marry fellow astronaut Steven Hawley. They remained married for about five years.

Although nothing could replace the excitement of Sally's first trip into space, her second flight might have been more enjoy-able because less of the attention was focused on her. Although she was the first American woman to make two trips to space, she was no longer the only American woman to have gone to space. Judith Resnik had gone to space in August 1984.

Sally wouldn't even be the only woman on Mission STS-41G. She would be flying with Kathryn Sullivan—and more atten-tion would be focused on Kathryn because she would be doing something no other American woman had ever done.

The *Challenger* took off once more, bright and early, from Kennedy Space Center on October 5, 1984, with its largest crew to date. There were seven astronauts onboard, again com-manded by Captain Robert Crippen. The launch was smooth without any problems.

A mission specialist again, Sally would assist with earth sci-ence experiments and operate the robotic arm in this mission, too. Within nine hours of the launch, she used the robotic arm to release the Earth Radiation Budget Satellite (ERBS). The sat-ellite would measure the incoming energy from the sun and the outgoing energy from Earth in addition to providing scientific observations of Earth.

Astronauts in space have a unique type of alarm clock. Mission Control often plays music before greeting the astronauts. On the first morning of Mission STS-41G, Mission Control said, "Good morning, *Challenger*. Houston standing by."

The standard response from the shuttle was to be "Roger." Instead, Sally, in a teasing mood, adopted the voice of an answering machine: "We're sorry, nobody can take your call right now. Please leave your name and number . . ."[7]

When the communications person at Mission Control replied with his name and phone number, the crew broke into laughter, and it became a running joke for the rest of the eight-day mission. It was a successful mission, and the *Challenger* landed where it had started, at Kennedy Space Center, on October 13, 1984.

Within the year, Sally was assigned to STS-61M mission training. She had begun her training when the next *Challenger* mission exploded after takeoff, killing everyone on board.

Sally was devastated. She knew these astronauts; many of them were her friends. She was appointed to the presidential commission that investigated the disaster and a redesign, which focused on the solid rockets, was recommended for the shuttle.

When the investigation was complete, Sally stayed in Washington, DC, working as special assistant to the administrator for NASA's long-range and strategic planning. While doing this, she wrote a report, "Leadership and America's Future in Space." The report recommended several things. One was a program called "Mission to Planet Earth," which would study the effects of natural and human-induced change on the Earth. Sally also recommended robotic planetary exploration, sending astronauts back to the moon, and sending astronauts to Mars in the future.

NASA created the Office of Exploration and appointed her its first director. The office was to focus on long-range planning, such as what would be needed for astronaut missions to Mars. Sally did this for a while before saying good-bye to NASA in 1987.

Another dream of Sally's was to be a professor of physics, which she accomplished on the San Diego campus of the University of California. She also conducted research, specifically theoretical work involving relativistic electron beams and intense radiation. While her work in physics was fulfilling, it wasn't enough. Sally wanted to reach kids, particularly breaking down barriers for girls in science and math education. She believed that science could enrich lives.

With this goal, Sally worked on an experiment that was part of Mission STS-93. Her work allowed middle school students, through a control center, to manipulate a digital camera mounted on the space shuttle. Later, she created EarthKAM, a NASA program that also worked with middle school kids. This time, the cameras were on the International Space Station. In 2011 the Gravity Recovery and Interior Laboratory (GRAIL) mission was launched to measure the moon's gravity. MoonKAMs on board gave classrooms access to pictures of the lunar surface from cameras on the spacecraft.

When tragedy struck again in 2003 with the *Columbia* shuttle, Sally volunteered her services once more. It was the 20th anniversary of her first flight into space. Sally was the only person to serve on both committees that investigated the *Challenger* and *Columbia* tragedies. She said, "It's rewarding because it's an opportunity to be part of the solution and part of the changes that will occur and will make the program better."[8]

With her partner, Tam O'Shaughnessy, Sally wrote five books on space for kids. (She also wrote three others with different coauthors.) Sally and Tam won the American Institute of

Physics's Science Writing Award in the children's category for *The Third Planet: Exploring the Earth from Space.*

Sally founded Sally Ride Science in 2001, a company that creates science programs and publications for upper elementary and middle school students. Sally Ride Science Clubs and Camps sprang up to support and encourage girls interested in science, technology, engineering, and math (STEM). In 2009, Sally joined with ExxonMobil to create the Sally Ride Science Academy to work with teachers and counselors to find ways to interest students in STEM careers. In three short years, more than 5,400 educators have been trained. Teachers trained at the academy loved learning how to use facts about the relevance of science in everyday life and incorporate the *Cool Careers in STEM* books—received during their training—as part of their lessons.

On July 23, 2012, people were surprised to hear that Sally Ride had died of pancreatic cancer. No one except for the people closest to her knew that she was sick. And that's the way she wanted it. She wanted attention focused on the many possibilities found in science, not on her.

President Obama stated, "Sally was a national hero and a powerful role model. She inspired generations of young girls to reach for the stars."[9]

NASA administrator Charles Bolden said, "Sally Ride broke barriers with grace and professionalism—and literally changed the face of America's space program. The nation has lost one of its finest leaders, teachers and explorers."[10]

Thanks to her final years, her legacy will live on to inspire and motivate generations to come.

LEARN MORE

Exploring Our Solar System by Sally Ride and Tam O'Shaughnessy (Crown Books, 2003).

Sally Ride Science. www.sallyridescience.com/.

Sally Ride: The First American Woman in Space by Tom Riddolls (Crabtree, 2010).

"Sally's Ride, 20 Years On." NASA. www.nasa.gov/home /hqnews/2003/jun/Ride_20_Anniv.html.

To Space and Back by Sally Ride and Susan Okie (Harper Collins, 1989).

"Who Was Sally Ride?" NASA. www.nasa.gov/audience /forstudents/k-4/stories/who-was-sally-ride-k4.html.

JUDITH RESNIK

....

ALL SHE EVER WANTED TO DO

I think something is only dangerous if you are not prepared for it, or if you don't have control over it, or if you can't think through how to get yourself out of a problem,"[1] said astronaut Dr. Judith Resnik. A year after Sally Ride's flight, Judy Resnik was flying on the first voyage of the space shuttle *Discovery.*

Her first flight, *Discovery* Mission STS-41D was to lift off on June 26, 1984, but a malfunctioning fuel valve started a fire. The launch was aborted, but *Discovery* took off two months later. The crew launched three satellites.

Judith Resnik enjoys low gravity with fellow crew members of the STS-41D mission (left to right): Michael Coats, Steven Hawley, Henry Hartsfield Jr., Richard Mullane, and Charles Walker. *NASA Images*

As a mission specialist, Judy assisted with experiments and tested a solar sail with the robotic arm. The crew performed photography experiments with an IMAX movie camera. After they used the robotic arm to remove a chunk of ice from the side of the space shuttle, the crew jokingly renamed themselves the "icebusters."

After 96 orbits around the Earth, the *Discovery* crew completed its mission. Judy had logged 144 hours and 57 minutes in space and was now considered a veteran astronaut. She told a crowd after returning home that she wanted to become a career astronaut and would stay as long as NASA wanted her.[2]

Judy was part of the same astronaut training group as Sally Ride. In fact, they were the two finalists for the first spaceflight by an American woman.

Born in Akron, Ohio, Judy enjoyed outdoor activities like bicycling and running. By the time she started elementary school, she could already read and do math. Because of this, she skipped kindergarten.

She was very close to her father, Marvin Resnik, an optometrist, who called his daughter *k'tanah*, which is Hebrew for "little one." They worked on electrical projects together when she was growing up. During her first spaceflight, a television camera captured a smiling Judy with a sign saying, "Hi, Dad." From her mother, Judy learned about discipline and piano; Judy became an accomplished classical pianist.

She was an excellent student and received a perfect score on her SATs. A member of the National Honor Society, Judy was a member of the chemistry, math, and French clubs. Staying busy helped her avoid her parent's arguing, but when she was 17, her parents divorced. Originally Judy was to live with her mother, but she preferred living with her father.

Judy graduated from Firestone High School as valedictorian of the class of 1966. She considered becoming a classical pianist but decided to pursue a bachelor of science degree in electrical engineering from Carnegie Mellon University. She later worked for a well-known electronics company, RCA (Radio Corporation of America) as a design engineer, performing circuit design for the missile and surface radar division while attending graduate school. Her work included the development of circuit designs for radar systems and space-related projects. She wrote a paper on design procedures for special-purpose integrated circuitry that caught the eye of NASA officials.

Judy returned to school as a biomedical engineer and staff fellow in the Laboratory of Neurophysiology at the National Institutes of Health in Bethesda, Maryland, from 1974 to 1977. There she performed biological research experiments concerning the physiology of visual systems. She received her PhD from the University of Maryland in 1977, the same year that NASA advertised for astronauts. She liked the idea of being an astronaut.

In 1978, while working as a senior systems engineer in product development with Xerox Corporation, Judy got the call that NASA wanted her. At 28 years of age, Judy, a biomedical engineer, left Xerox in California for the Johnson Space Center in Houston. She took flying lessons, receiving almost perfect scores on her pilot's exam. Like Sally, Judy completed her one-year training by August 1979. She loved being there. Soon, the other astronauts were calling her J.R.

While waiting to be selected for a flight, she worked on orbiter development, including experimental software, the Remote Manipulator System (RMS), and training techniques. After six years, she was named to the first *Discovery* crew.

Judy liked dealing with the press even less than Sally did. She was the "Jewish astronaut" or the "second woman." But she said, "I don't want to be a Jewish astronaut, I just want to be an astronaut, period."[3]

In 1986, Judy was ready for her second mission. It would be in the *Challenger* and the 25th shuttle launch for the United States. Judy, again a mission specialist, would use the robotic arm to install a tracking and data relay satellite. The satellite would hopefully improve communication for future space shuttles. She would also deploy a data relay satellite that would track Halley's Comet, which was on its every-75-years visit near the sun (and Earth).

Now that the excitement of being the second American woman in space and the first Jewish astronaut was over, she just wanted to enjoy the flight. Besides, attention was being focused on the first teacher in space, Christa McAuliffe, she was also assigned to the mission. The crew for Mission STS-51L would truly be a multicultural crew. In addition to the "Jewish astronaut," an African American astronaut and an Asian American astronaut were also part of the two-woman, five-man crew.

Some people later questioned the launch of the shuttle, which had already been subjected to many delays. Just the day before the launch, there was a four-hour delay because of a problem with a bolt in the handle of the shuttle door. It took two hours to remove the bolt and repair it. By the time that was complete, high winds gusting up to 30 mph prevented the launch. Launches never took place if wind speeds were greater than 17 mph.

In all, six postponements delayed the shuttle launch. Half had been due to weather. The other delays included problems with the landing sites.

The new launch was scheduled for 9:38 AM on Tuesday, January 28, 1986. Freezing temperatures overnight were predicted, which was unusual for Florida's Kennedy Space Center. At 15 degrees colder than any other space launch, the temperature concerned some NASA officials. But there was also a lot of pressure to make the launch happen because the launch window—related to the weather and future scheduled spaceflights—was just about at its end. *Challenger* was supposed to launch two satellites. Millions of Americans, particularly schoolchildren, would also be watching Christa, the first teacher in space, teach two lessons.

Early Tuesday morning, Judy smiled and waved before climbing into the *Challenger*. The launch did take place, although it was two hours later than expected.

"LVLH," said Dr. Judith Resnik, mission specialist for the *Challenger* Mission STS-51L. LVLH stood for "local vertical–local horizontal." She was reminding the crew about a cockpit switch change 14 seconds after takeoff. It was the last thing anyone heard from her.

In the next minute, Commander Francis Scobee and pilot Michael J. Smith were heard by Mission Control discussing the wind. They were monitoring the speed of the shuttle as it went from Mach .5 to Mach .9. The winds began altering the flight path as they reached Mach 1, the speed of sound.

The pilot throttled up the shuttle engines. A flame leaked from the booster rocket, but the astronauts didn't know that. No one did because everything was happening quickly. By the time the ship reached 35,000 feet at Mach 1.5, the flame had eaten through the booster's support. An explosion caused the space shuttle to tilt to the right, and Mission Control heard Smith say, "Uh-oh."

A brilliant flash erupted and grew until 73 seconds after the launch. Black smoke and an orange flame came from the right rocket booster. The *Challenger* ship broke up, with pieces hitting the nearby ocean at a strong impact. The *Challenger* space shuttle was gone, along with every member of its crew.

The shuttle disaster was related to the O-rings in the rocket boosters. They didn't work well in cold weather, which allowed one to leak explosive gases. When the intense flame burned through it, the shuttle exploded. The space program was brought to a halt as NASA worked on fixing the program. Fourteen women remained on NASA's active astronaut rosters.

Judy's memorial was held on February 3, 1986, back home in Akron, Ohio. Senator John Glenn spoke at the service. Her hometown honored her memory by opening the Judith A. Resnik Center for Women's Health and by offering scholarships in her name. The Judith Resnik Challenger Scholarship is available to women at Carnegie Mellon University who major in computer science, engineering, or science.

Judy had received a NASA Space Flight Medal after her first flight, the highest honor given by NASA. After her death, she was awarded the Congressional Space Medal of Honor.

Perhaps what Judy would appreciate most, due to her love of space, was that a star, an asteroid, and craters on the moon and on Venus are all named after her.

The Challenger Center for Space Science Education

The Challenger Center for Space Science Education was created by the families of the *Challenger* crew to honor the astronauts by continuing their legacy to explore, discover, and teach. The first Challenger Learning Center opened in Houston in August 1988 to encourage children's interests in science and technology. Today, there are 45 such centers throughout the world. The centers allow children to solve real-world problems as astronauts and engineers. Almost a half million middle school students and teachers have passed through their doors.

LEARN MORE

Challenger Center for Space Science Education. www .challenger.org.

"The Crew of the *Challenger* Shuttle." NASA. http://history .nasa.gov/Biographies/challenger.html.

"Remarks of Senator John Glenn, Memorial Service for Judith Resnik." NASA. www.nasa.gov/centers/glenn /about/memorial.html.

The Space Shuttle Challenger *Disaster in American History* by Suzanne Lieurance (Enslow, 2001).

Wings and Rockets: The Story of Women in Air and Space by Jeannine Atkins (Farrar, Straus and Giroux, 2003).

KATHRYN SULLIVAN

....

A WALK INTO HISTORY

On the East Coast of the United States, the sun was high in the sky at 11 AM. Millions of miles away, astronaut Dr. Kathryn Sullivan was entering an airlock on the space shuttle *Challenger* along with Lieutenant Commander David Leestma of the navy. Sullivan, known as Kathy to her friends, toted a tool case with ten implements in it. The two astronauts worked their way to the end of the payload bay.

Standing up straight in the payload bay, Kathy got her first direct look at Earth and the stars without a window in between. It was the view of a lifetime. Attached to each other and the space shuttle, the astronauts took their first steps into space at 11:46 AM.

Kathryn Sullivan on her second spaceflight. *NASA*

"That is really great," Kathy said.[1]

Soon, the safety lines demanded their attention. They were getting tangled, but 32-year-old Kathy wasn't about to let that ruin her experience. She was doing what only a handful of other astronauts had done—she was walking in space. Kathy was the first American woman to take this walk, known technically as an extravehicular activity (EVA).

The main goal for the day's EVA for Mission STS-41G was to attach the valves necessary for a fuel transfer to a satellite the next day. If they were able to successfully refuel satellites, they would no longer have to abandon them in space as litter.

Kathy managed the tools and took pictures as Leestma installed a one-way ball valve in the satellite for the rocket fuel to flow into. After the valve was installed, Leestma hooked a hose up to the valve from the huge refueling test stand in the cargo bay. The rocket fuel hydrazine is extremely unstable and can explode if heated or overpressurized. The next day, a remote-control transfer from inside the ship would be attempted.

After slightly more than an hour, their main objective was completed. They then moved to the front of the space shuttle to work on a wobbly communications antenna. A problem that had occurred earlier in the week meant the antenna couldn't go in certain directions.

Kathy took the lead in fixing the antenna while Leestma handled the tools and the camera. He asked whether it was time for lunch. As she manually aligned the antenna, Kathy answered, "I bet they ate our lunch."

Inside the ship, fellow crew member Dr. Sally Ride jokingly confirmed their suspicions. "Hey, you'd have loved it."[2]

In order to keep the antenna from thrashing around on the way back to Earth, Kathy drove two locking pins into it. One other item on the to-do list was inspecting the shuttle imaging radar. In taking pictures of Earth, the radar saw things invisible to the human eye. Earlier in the week, Kathy and Sally had used the shuttle's robotic arm to squeeze the panels shut when they wouldn't latch on their own. Kathy noted the thickness of insulation on the panels. The panels were wider than she was tall and more than six times her height.

The crew and NASA needed to decide whether to try to use the shuttle imaging radar again. They feared that if the panels were opened, they might not close again. And if the panels didn't work right, they wouldn't be able to fly to a lower orbit. The radar was something that Kathy had worked on while on Earth, so she knew it well. Kathy confirmed that the shuttle

Shuttle Imaging Radar

• •

One of the best ways to control malaria is by looking at Earth from space not with the human eye, but with a special camera. In the 1980s, NASA sent the shuttle imaging radar on a shuttle flight. It took pictures with radar, which can photograph in the dark and through bad weather, and can see things that the human eye can't.

That's why the special camera eye was used over tropical areas. It was looking for mosquito-breeding sites. If these sites could be located and destroyed, it would help control malaria, one of the most serious and common diseases in tropical areas. Shuttle imaging radar has also been used to locate ancient river channels under the Sahara Desert and to create topographic maps of Earth and Venus.

imaging radar could be used again and that, this time, the panels would shut easily.

As Kathy and David finished the EVA, they noted a safety cap flying off the hatch of the airlock as they started to climb in. Commander Crippen, piloting his fourth space shuttle flight, fired the thrusters so that they could get the cap. They did, and after a spacewalk that lasted three and a half hours, they returned to the shuttle cabin.

The crew later talked to President Reagan via satellite. Kathy told the president that the spacewalk "was the most fantastic experience of my life."

The next day, the *Challenger* crew successfully performed a remote-control transfer of about 30 gallons of rocket fuel. It was the first gas station in space.

Other projects for the eight-day flight included deploying an energy-monitoring satellite that measured the amount of solar energy the Earth's atmosphere reflected into space. This would aid weather forecasts.

But refueling the satellite was one of the last projects completed before the space shuttle and its seven-person crew returned home. Their final goal was to land at Kennedy Space Center. If they were able to, it would only be the second time in the history of the shuttle program. Weather conditions often required space shuttles to land at Edwards Air Force Base in California. When that happened, it took extra time—about a week—to get the spacecraft back to Florida. With a busy schedule of monthly shuttle launches, NASA needed that time to look over the shuttle and make any repairs.

The *Challenger* came in over the central United States for the first time. It descended at 15 times the speed of sound, flying over Minnesota, Wisconsin, Indiana, and Ohio. On its way to Florida, it continued descending over Kentucky, Tennessee, and

Georgia until it reached Florida and became visible. After landing three miles from its launch site, Mission Control announced, "The largest crew in the history of space flight is home."

For mission specialist Dr. Kathryn Sullivan, a geologist from the original group of six women, it was just the beginning of a long and successful career that continues today. After the flight, the president appointed her to the National Commission on Space.

Although Kathy was born in New Jersey, she considered Woodland Hills, California, her home. This is where she grew up. As Kathy and Sally Ride got to know each other, they realized that they had been in first grade together at Hayvenhurst Elementary School, although neither really remembered much.

Kathy's interest in space came naturally; her father was an aerospace design engineer with the Lockheed Corporation. After graduating from the University of California–Santa Cruz with a degree in earth sciences, Kathy went on to earn a doctorate in geology from Dalhousie University in Nova Scotia, Canada. In addition to speaking five foreign languages, Kathy Sullivan is an accomplished mountain climber and a private pilot with power and glider aircraft ratings.

Before joining NASA, she participated in oceanography expeditions for the US Geological Survey. At NASA, Kathy's research was on planetary geology and remote sensing. As a systems engineer operator in NASA's high-altitude research aircraft, she participated in several remote sensing projects in Alaska.

After two more flights as a mission specialist, on Missions STS-31 and STS-45, Kathy retired from NASA in 1992. She had logged 532 hours in space. Kathy's 1990 mission on STS-31 launched the *Hubble* Space Telescope into orbit. For her last mission in 1992, she served as payload commander on the first Spacelab mission dedicated to NASA's Mission to Planet Earth.

The mission concentrated on gathering data that would improve the understanding of Earth's climate. When not in space, Kathy worked as an oceanographer for the US Navy Reserve.

President Bush appointed her as chief scientist at the National Oceanic and Atmospheric Administration (NOAA). In her position, she oversaw research and technology programs on topics that ranged from climate change to marine biodiversity.

She went on to a wide variety of educational positions, from heading an organization that strengthened science in the classroom to teaching at Ohio State University. Kathy has received countless honors and appointments to commissions.

On May 2, 2011, Kathy returned to NOAA. President Obama appointed her as the assistant secretary of commerce for environmental observation and prediction and the deputy administrator. She was confirmed unanimously by the US Senate. On February 28, 2013, she was promoted to acting undersecretary of commerce for oceans and atmosphere as well as acting NOAA administrator.

In addition to leading NOAA, Kathy's work involves making decisions about satellites, space weather, water, and climate science as they will best benefit Americans.

LEARN MORE

"Kathryn D. Sullivan." NASA Johnson Center Oral History Project. www.jsc.nasa.gov/history/oral_histories /SullivanKD/SullivanKD_5-10-07.htm.

"Meet Kathy Sullivan." NASA. http://quest.arc.nasa.gov /space/frontiers/sullivan.html.

Women in Space by Carole S. Briggs (Lerner, 1998).

SHANNON LUCID

....

A RUSSIAN FAVORITE

Imagine living millions of miles from home for four and a half months. At your temporary home, the people speak little of your language, and you're not a native speaker of their language. Oh, and your main diet is dehydrated food. As you get close to the days when you will see your family and friends again, you are told that there's a problem and you must stay for six more weeks.

If you're astronaut Dr. Shannon Lucid, you're thankful that you have plenty of books to read and that Sunday is Jell-O Night. You also plan what you're going to eat when you return home, including things like potato chips, M&Ms, and junk food.

Shannon Lucid stayed in shape with the treadmill at the *Mir* Space Station. *NASA*

Shannon Lucid was the oldest of the original six American women astronauts and the last of the group to make a spaceflight, but she became one of the most famous astronauts of all time, setting many records as a woman and as an American in space.

Before Shannon embarked on 188 days aboard the *Mir* Space Station with two Russian cosmonauts, she was already a veteran astronaut with four other flights under her belt. Her first flight was in 1985 as a mission specialist on the *Discovery* space shuttle. She also flew on two Atlantis missions and a Columbia mission. She was part of missions that deployed satellites and the *Galileo* spacecraft to explore Jupiter. NASA called *Columbia* Mission STS-58 one of its most successful Spacelab flights, as the crew performed extensive medical experiments on themselves and on 48 rats in order to learn about human and animal physiology in space.

Yet the spaceflight that Shannon Lucid is most known for is her fifth, last, and longest mission. On March 22, 1996, Shannon boarded the *Atlantis* STS-76 flight. Her destination was the Russian Space Station, *Mir*. She took the place of Dr. Norman Thagard, the astronaut who held the American record for the longest single period in space. On July 15, she broke his record. By September 7, she had spent more time in space than any woman in the world, breaking the record set by Russian cosmonaut Elena Kondakova.

Two days after the launch of the *Atlantis*, Shannon moved into the *Mir* Space Station, which she would share with cosmonauts Yuri Onufrienko, commander of the space station, and Yuri Usachev, the flight engineer. According to Shannon, "They acted very happy to see me. I believe that they really were. So as soon as the hatch opened, I moved over and became part of the Mir-21 crew."[1]

Shannon would be the first American woman to spend time on *Mir*, and there were concerns about what she might face due to the rumored sexism of Russian men. Although the deputy commander of the Gagarin Cosmonaut Training Center at Star City had commented that the two male cosmonauts would welcome Shannon because women loved to clean, she reported that they all worked together to keep the space station clean. She reported no problems with her crewmates, although she questioned the need for military command once the International Space Station was up and running. Since the military-versus-civilian discussion had been going since the first days of space exploration, it was welcome feedback for NASA.

As the board engineer, Shannon conducted scientific research as she had for previous missions. Just as important to NASA was that she learn how to manage a space station and be a good diplomat with the Russians she would work with. She did this beyond anyone's expectations.

The missions to *Mir* would be beneficial when they started building the International Space Station. Shannon's positive attitude and humor made her a favorite with the two Yuris and the Russian Space Agency.

The three astronauts conversed in Russian, although Shannon admitted to a limited command of the language, which made it sometimes difficult to communicate. Yet in August, when NASA reported finding evidence of ancient Martian life, it "filled up a whole conversation for us at supper time."

What's it like living in space for six months? For personal hygiene, she lived on sponge baths and space shampoo. (This rinseless shampoo was originally made for hospitals where it was used for patients who couldn't take showers.) The weightlessness from low gravity causes a loss of muscle tone, making exercise very important, so Shannon ran on a treadmill. Much of her time was spent in the Base Block, which was where Shannon and the cosmonauts talked to Mission Control and ate their meals. While the two Yuris slept in the Base Block, Shannon slept in the *Spektr* module.

Shannon made Sundays special. It was the day she often talked with her family, so she decided to have other fun Sunday rituals such as wearing pink socks. Perhaps the one thing all three astronauts enjoyed about Sundays was the Jell-O. Before taking her flight, Shannon had asked the people at Houston's Johnson Space Center if they could put Jell-O in a drink bag. They did, providing her with a variety of flavors. After adding hot water, the astronauts put the Jell-O in the refrigerator and later ate it as a special treat on Sundays.

Shannon talked to NASA staff regularly, usually twice a day. She kept in contact with her family via e-mail and biweekly video link-ups. Shannon was able to telephone her 81-year-old mother on her birthday and have a Mother's Day video chat with her family. In her free time, she engaged in one of her favorite pastimes, reading. Not only had she brought up reading material, but her family also sent boxes of books on the supply ships.

A typical day on *Mir* began around 8 AM, Moscow time, which was midnight at Johnson Space Center in Houston. The day was filled with experiments, research, and observations of Earth. Some of Shannon's experiments included long-term protein crystal growth and embryonic development of a quail egg in microgravity. Of the 28 experiments she was assigned, all but one yielded results that increased knowledge. The one failure was due to an equipment issue. Later, she studied changes in plants in microgravity, a potentially useful experiment since it's believed that plants could contribute to supporting life in space, because they provide oxygen and take away carbon dioxide.

In May, the cosmonauts began going on spacewalks to work on *Priroda*, the seventh and last module for the *Mir* Space Station. The cosmonauts joked about how she was commander during these times. While they worked on the outside of *Priroda*, Shannon worked on the inside of the module. Often Shannon would have hot tea or a tube of juice waiting for them after their long work sessions. Once, however, she mistakenly put out ketchup instead of juice.

The three-member crew celebrated Cosmonautics Day on April 12, the anniversary of the flight of Yuri Gagarin, the first man sent to space. They joined to watch movies together, both English and Russian-dubbed movies. They especially enjoyed adventure movies, and *Apollo 13* was a particular favorite.

Occasionally, all three took part in press conferences through a two-way video link. Russian high school students asked questions in a radio hookup with *Mir*, including what Russian drink Shannon liked best (her answer: cherry). In another linkup, when Shannon was asked how the crew was getting along, she said, "I think maybe we laugh a little more together now than we did at the very beginning because we're more comfortable with each other and we understand each other."[2]

Something that they all looked forward to was the arrival of the *Progress*. The *Progress* was an unmanned supply ship that brought food, supplies, mail, and equipment. And not just dehydrated food, but also fresh food like apples, oranges, and tomatoes. Shannon's family sent her a bag of snack food and a box of books.

August 19 was Shannon's 150th day in space. Company arrived when the *Soyuz* TM-24 docked with *Mir*, bringing two more Russian cosmonauts plus French astronaut Claudie André-Deshays. Days later, Shannon said good-bye to Claudie and the two Yuris, who took the *Soyuz* back to Earth, and she got to know two more cosmonauts, Valery Korzun and Aleksandr Kaleri, for the remainder of her stay.

Shannon's return to Earth was delayed first by problems with the booster rockets on the shuttle. Once that was resolved, Hurricane Fran delayed the space shuttle launch that was scheduled to pick her up. The delays meant that Shannon missed the birthdays of two of her children. But on September 18, the *Atlantis* STS-79 docked with the *Mir* space station. Shannon had a big smile on her face as she greeted her replacement, John E. Blaha.

An American Pioneer

Shannon's life of adventure started soon after she was born. She was born Shannon Wells to American missionaries on January 14, 1943, in Shanghai, China. When she was only six weeks old, she and her parents were captured by the Japanese and held as prisoners of war for a year during the Second Sino-Japanese War.

Upon leaving China, her family settled in Bethany, Oklahoma, a suburb of Oklahoma City. One of her favorite parts of school was hearing and reading about American pioneers, which fueled her love of exploring. Despite the prejudice against women in the sciences, she attended the University of Oklahoma where she earned a bachelor's degree in chemistry and a masters and PhD in biochemistry. She worked as a chemist until chosen for the space program. Shannon still enjoys flying and is a commercial, instrument, and multiengine-rated pilot.

Shannon landed at Kennedy Space Center on September 26, 1996, after staying longer in space for one mission than any other American had ever done. When the space shuttle landed at 8:13 AM, she surprised everyone by walking out on her own two feet. It was the first time her body had felt gravity in six months. She did show a loss of calcium and muscle strength from her trip, but this was expected.

President Clinton awarded Shannon the Congressional Space Medal of Honor after the *Mir* mission. She was the ninth person and first woman to receive the award. He called her "a terrific inspiration for young women around the country and all around the world" and gave her a large box of M&Ms. The Russian president, Boris Yeltsin, presented her with the highest honor a non-Russian can receive, the Order of Friendship Medal.

After her five spaceflights, Shannon worked as NASA's chief scientist in Washington, DC, and at the Astronaut Office at Johnson Space Center in Houston. She retired from NASA in January 2012.

LEARN MORE

Astronauts, Athletes, and Ambassadors: Oklahoma Women from 1950–2007 by Glenda Carlile (New Forums Press, 2007).

"Interview: Shannon Lucid." NASA. www.nasa.gov/50th /50th_magazine/lucid.html.

Shannon Lucid: Space Ambassador by Carmen Bredeson (Gateway, 2000).

"Shannon W. Lucid. National Women's Hall of Fame." www.greatwomen.org/women-of-the-hall/search-the -hall/details/2/100-Lucid.

MAE JEMISON

·············

DOCTOR ASTRONAUT

During the late 1960s and early '70s, many of the Apollo and Gemini spaceflights were broadcast on television. Schools and homes throughout the nation were tuned in to America's many firsts in space travel. One of the many viewers was a young girl growing up on Chicago's South Side. It didn't matter to her that the astronauts were white men and that she was an African American girl. She knew that someday she would be the one flying into space.

Jump ahead to September 12, 1992. The space shuttle *Endeavour* is launched for Mission STS-47 at 10:23 AM from Kennedy Space Center in Florida. As the 50th space shuttle launch for

Astronauts Dr. N. Jan Davis (left) and **Dr. Mae C. Jemison** (right) as mission specialists on board the STS-47 mission. *NASA*

NASA, it's also the first since 1985 to take place on time. The perfect conditions were a good omen for the seven crew members onboard under commander Robert "Hoot" Gibson.

It was a spaceflight of many firsts. The *Endeavour's* STS-47 mission included America's first married couple flying together. Although there have been several instances of married couples who are both astronauts, this flight marked the first time that a couple—Dr. N. Jan Davis and Lieutenant Colonel Mark C. Lee—had flown together. Additionally, Dr. Mamoru Mohri was the first Japanese astronaut to fly on an American spacecraft.

Most meaningful to many Americans was that the *Endeavour* also carried the first African American female astronaut, Dr. Mae Jemison, who was living her dream. Before the flight, she told reporters, "I'm extremely excited to be on the flight because it's something that I wanted to do since I was a small child."[1]

Mae Jemison, born in Decatur, Alabama, moved to Chicago as a young child. She was the youngest of three children whose parents valued education. Charlie Jemison was a roofer and carpenter who worked multiple jobs. When they first moved to Chicago, Mae's mother, Dorothy Green Jemison, had two years of college and did odd jobs. But she went back to school, finishing at Chicago Teachers College and becoming an elementary school teacher.

Mae gravitated to science early, reading about astronomy and enjoying science fiction novels. When she told her kindergarten teacher that she wanted to be a scientist some day, the teacher corrected her.

"You mean a nurse," the teacher said.[2] No, Mae didn't mean a nurse. She meant a scientist, perhaps a scientist who would go into space. She knew she could do it, even if the people around her didn't. She became used to breaking stereotypes.

Also important in her life was dance. She began taking lessons at the age of nine, starting a lifelong love of dance. People often remark that science and dance don't seem to go together, but Mae disagrees. "I consider them both to be expressions of the boundless creativity that people have to share with one another."[3]

Mae graduated from high school early at age 16. She went to Stanford University and declared a double major, African American Studies and Chemical Engineering. African American females were a new sight in Stanford's engineering department in the mid-1970s, and Mae confronted both racism and sexism. After graduating, she continued her education at Cornell Medical College. During her summers, she provided healthcare in places like Thailand, Cuba, and Kenya.

Mae spent several years as a doctor in the Peace Corps. She worked in the Western African countries of Sierra Leone and Liberia. She entered private practice in Los Angeles in 1985 while taking graduate engineering courses. Sally Ride's spaceflight in 1983 reignited Mae's love of space. Ride's first flight was also the first flight for an African American male, Guion S. Bluford Jr.

After applying for the astronaut program, Mae became an astronaut in 1987. Her class of 92 astronaut contained 16 women and 4 African American men. She was the only African American female.

Endeavour mission STS-47 took about eight minutes to reach the Earth's orbit. For the last few minutes, Mae and the other astronauts felt a lot of pressure across their chests. But once in orbit, Mae enjoyed the sensation of floating. When Mae looked outside the shuttle, she noticed a beautiful glow surrounding the Earth.[4] It was the Earth's atmosphere.

Once in orbit, the crew of two women and five men first activated the pressurized laboratory known as Spacelab-J. Located

Science in Space

The late 1980s and early '90s were busy years with strong science-focused missions into space. The first Spacelab Life Sciences mission, STS-40, began its nine-day flight on June 21, 1991. Almost half of the crew was female, and it was the first time ever that three women had traveled together on a spaceflight. Physician Margaret Rhea Seddon was the veteran of the group. She was joined by astrophysician Tammy Jernigan and biochemist Millie Hughes-Fulford.

in the shuttle cargo bay, the bus-sized lab would be the location of many of the 43 experiments scheduled for the spaceflight.

As a mission specialist who was both a chemical engineer and a physician, Mae was largely responsible for reproduction studies and the use of biofeedback techniques in space adaption syndrome. About 80 percent of astronauts suffered from space sickness or motion sickness in space. For the motion sickness experiment, Mae tested herself. Unlike the other astronauts, she did not take medication to prevent motion sickness. Instead, she used biofeedback techniques to consciously control her heartbeat and skin temperature. She was successful, but more experimentation on others would have to be performed.

The reproductive studies involved frogs. Mae removed eggs from four female South African clawed frogs. She fertilized the eggs with sperm. Three days later, approximately a hundred tadpoles were born. Mae observed their development in space through the remainder of the eight-day flight and was able to bring the tadpoles—conceived and born in space—back to Earth.

Astronauts are allowed to bring a few personal items to space. As a dancer and occasional choreographer, Mae brought a poster from the noted Alvin Ailey American Dance Theater.

Space Sickness

Have you ever had motion sickness? This condition develops in some people during motion. Other names for it are seasickness, air sickness, and car sickness. This occurs when what the eyes see doesn't match what the body feels. Nausea and dizziness are common effects of motion sickness.

Space sickness is motion sickness in space, and more than half of the people who go to space develop it. Why so many? Possibly because the limited gravity makes it challenging to figure out which way is up and which way is down. Another name for space sickness is space adaptation syndrome. For many who develop space sickness, the symptoms go away in a day or two as the body and senses get used to the unique environment of space.

Another way to overcome space sickness before a flight is to spend some time in low-gravity situations. A KC-135 airplane uses parabolic arcs to create periods of weightlessness. But most people know the plane by another name—the vomit comet.

While in medical school, Mae had continued taking dance at the Ailey School. Space, like dance, has no limits.

She also brought West African art objects to symbolize that space belongs to all nations. Since leaving NASA, Mae has worked on teaching others that space is indeed a birthright of everyone who is on this planet.[5]

Dartmouth College agreed. They offered Mae a fellowship to live in New Hampshire and lecture at the college. Mae also began teaching a course on space technology and developing countries. The course focused on using satellite and telecommunications technology to improve healthcare in West Africa. People from all over the campus—including those from the Ivy League school's engineering, English, religion, and government departments—signed up for Mae's course.

More recently, Mae's foundation, the Dorothy Jemison Foundation for Excellence (named after her mother), received a $500,000 grant from the US government to form the 100 Year Starship project. The proposal focuses on making interstellar space travel a reality within the next 100 years.

The principle behind the project follows what Dr. Mae Jemison has lived by and has tried to communicate to others throughout her life: "Don't be limited by others' limited imaginations."[6]

LEARN MORE

"Astronaut Mae Jemison." NASA. www.nasa.gov/audience/forstudents/k-4/home/F_Astronaut_Mae_Jemison.html.

Dr. Mae Jemison website. www.drmae.com.

"Dr. Mae Jemison." NASA. http://starchild.gsfc.nasa.gov/docs/StarChild/whos_who_level2/jemison.html.

Mae Jemison by Sonia Black (Mondo, 2000).

Mae Jemison: Out of This World by Corinne J. Naden and Rose Blue (Millbrook Press, 2003).

ELLEN OCHOA

·················

CAREER ASTRONAUT

The space shuttle *Discovery* carried special cargo on Mission STS-56. Sitting in the shuttle's cargo bay was the 2,800-pound *Spartan* satellite. On day three of the flight, mission specialist Dr. Ellen Ochoa used the *Discovery*'s robotic arm to place *Spartan* in a separate orbit from the space shuttle. In two days time, the *Discovery* would rendezvous with the satellite. Ellen, an electrical engineer, would use the remote manipulation system arm again to retrieve the *Spartan*, which would be filled with data about the sun's corona and the charged particles, known as the solar wind, that affect the Earth.

Ellen Ochoa practices an emergency shuttle exit for Mission STS-56. *NASA Johnson Space Center*

During Ellen's second mission on the *Atlantis*, the shuttle carried the Atmospheric Laboratory for Applications and Science (ATLAS). The purpose of ATLAS was to study the sun's energy during an 11-year solar cycle and its effect on Earth. The crew would gather information about the ozone and how changes in the sun affected the Earth's climate. Ellen again retrieved an atmosphere research satellite at the end of the flight. She also served as payload commander.

She was in her element. Her work before and since joining NASA focused on optical systems that processed information. She had, in fact, invented an optical inspection system, an optical object recognition system, and a system for removing noise from images.

As the first Hispanic woman in space, Ellen had come a long way from growing up as one of five children in La Mesa,

Jobs in Space

Space exploration is a big job that requires many people. Even the astronauts have different jobs. These are some of the most common jobs for astronauts:

Commander: The commander of a space shuttle or space station is basically the boss. A space shuttle commander must also be an expert pilot because he or she carries out the transfers, such as dockings. The commander also brings the ship back to Earth from space.

(continued on the next page)

Pilot: The pilot flies the shuttle most of the time and serves as an assistant pilot when the commander takes the controls.

Mission Specialist: A mission specialist is an astronaut and a scientist who must know about everything on the shuttle: shuttle operations, safety, crew planning, and experiments. If there's not enough food for the trip, the mission specialist is the person to blame.

Payload Specialist: Unlike the mission specialist, the payload specialist is usually assigned to a specific experiment or groups of experiments. Often the experiment comes from where the payload specialist works—a university, research center, government agency, or corporation—or from another country. This person does not have to be an astronaut.

Payload Commander: The payload commander is an astronaut who is in charge of coordinating all the experiments. When some missions have 50 or even 80 experiments, you can see that this is a very important job.

Flight Engineer: The flight engineer assists the commander and the pilot and otherwise assumes many of the duties of the mission specialist.

Capcom: The capcom (short for "capsule communicator") is an astronaut who stays grounded. The capcom communicates with the shuttle crew from Mission Control.

California. When she was in fifth grade, she wanted to be president, but she also liked music, which became her first major at San Diego State University. Ellen changed her major five times, finally graduating with a degree in physics, although she remained a classical flutist, as well.

While Ellen pursued a master of science degree at Stanford University, NASA announced the first spaceflights that would include women astronauts. As Ellen worked on her PhD in electrical engineering, Sally Ride made history.

Ellen's thoughts turned to space. If other women could go into space, why not her? When she finally applied to NASA, she was accepted for training at the age of 32. She became part of the class of 1990 along with Eileen Collins. The following year, Ellen completed the training. She spent half of her time training for upcoming missions and the other half completing various assignments, including crew representative, lead shuttle communications for Mission Control, and other jobs.

In 1999, Ellen served as a mission specialist again on Mission STS-96. The Discovery became the first shuttle to dock with the new International Space Station (ISS). Using the arm, Ellen coordinated and moved equipment from the space shuttle to the space station. The equipment—computers, medical supplies, clothing, and food—would be used for the first crew to live and work at the ISS.

The 10-day mission wasn't without its problems. Of particular concern were the headaches and nausea suffered by some of the crew. Although none of it was severe, NASA investigated and found that it seemed to come from one of the modules of the space station, a workstation built by Russia. NASA recommended monitoring the air supply and forcing more fresh air into the module; if that didn't work, they might need to redo the ductwork.

For Ellen's last mission into space, she served as flight engineer for the *Atlantis* space shuttle. Mission STS-110 had the same destination as her previous mission, the ISS. This time, they would bring the ISS a backbone and part of a railroad.

The backbone, a 44-foot-long truss, would serve as part of a support beam for the space station. Ellen used the robotic arm of the ISS, called the Canadarm, instead of the shuttle's robotic arm to install the truss. The Canadarm worked like a human arm with the operator—in this case, Ellen—working the arm through the viewing of cameras and monitors. Although the Canadarm had experienced previous problems, it worked perfectly under Ellen's experienced hands. The 27,000-pound truss was attached to the American-made *Destiny* science module of the station. When complete, the truss would be 356 feet long. It contained 475,000 parts, including many electronic components, such as a television system to view the outside work. Crew members went on a space walk to finish the attachment process and connect the power and data cable hookups.

Ellen also used the arm to move the astronauts outside the space station. The railroad, a mobile transport platform, would be used to transport astronauts across the station for future construction and repairs.

After four flights and 978 hours in space, Ellen moved to working on the other side of operations. At Mission Control, she served as director of flight crew operations and later deputy director at Johnson Space Center.

As director of flight crew operations, she was in Mission Control when they first got word that the space shuttle *Columbia* had disintegrated over Texas upon reentry into the atmosphere. Upon hearing the news, Ellen closed her eyes and said, "Oh, God." When the crash was confirmed, she kept busy providing services to families of the *Columbia* astronauts.

Ellen is frequently asked to speak to Hispanic youth. It's something she gladly does. Her father, whose family was from Mexico, didn't speak Spanish in their home when Ellen was growing up. He believed people would be prejudiced against his children if they spoke Spanish. She's happy that this is less true today and is proud of her Hispanic heritage.

KNOW MORE

Ellen Ochoa by Annie Buckley (Cherry Lake Publishing, 2007).

Extraordinary Hispanic Americans by Cesar Alegre (Children's Press, 2007).

"Innovative Lives, Research in Orbit." Smithsonian Institution. http://invention.smithsonian.org/centerpieces /ilives/lecture07.html.

"Inventor of the Week: Ellen Ochoa." MIT. http://web .mit.edu/invent/iow/ochoa.html.

"Latina Women of NASA: Ellen Ochoa, Ph.D." NASA. http://oeop.larc.nasa.gov/hep/lwon/LWONbios/jsc -EOchoa.html.

EILEEN COLLINS

....

SPACE SHUTTLE COMMANDER

By 1995, there were plans to begin creating an International Space Station in 1997. It would be bigger and better than the American space station *Skylab* and the Russian Space Station *Mir*. But the project would first start with a joint space mission between the two superpowers of spaceflight. The space shuttle *Discovery* would take Mission STS-63, the 67th space shuttle flight, to *Mir*, perched 200 miles away in Earth's orbit. The *Discovery* would be the first space shuttle to dock with *Mir*.

Although there had been a joint flight in the 1970s, working together wasn't something that either country was used to. Mission STS-63 would be the beginning.

Space Shuttle Commander **Eileen Collins** reviewing a checklist while seated at the flight deck commander's station in the *Columbia* space shuttle. *NASA*

Soon after midnight on February 3, 1995, *Discovery* launched into the night sky with a six-person crew that included the second Russian to fly on a NASA shuttle. They had met their first challenge—liftoff during the five-minute window required for *Discovery* to meet *Mir*.

An excellent pilot needed to bring the 122-foot-long winged *Discovery* spacecraft within 30 feet of the slightly smaller *Mir* space station. That pilot was Colonel Eileen Collins, the first woman to pilot a spacecraft. She carried the hopes and dreams of many with her.

Her parents were in the stands along with members of the Mercury 13. Eileen was aware that she owed so much to the women who passed the astronaut testing more than thirty years ago. From them, Eileen learned that "it's important that young women see they have role models and see they can be astronauts."

Eileen had invited the 11 surviving female trainee astronauts to the launch and offered to carry mementos to space. Seven women were able to come; one stated that Eileen carried "our dreams" into space.

Back home in Elmira, New York, many residents in the small town of 30,000 stayed up late so they could see one of their own make history. Located in southern New York near the border with Pennsylvania, the town's main claim to fame was being the final resting place of literary great Mark Twain—until that day, when Eileen Collins flew into space. Watching on television, the mayor held his breath until the *Discovery* successfully separated from the rocket boosters. He wasn't the only one. The next morning the town newspaper, the *Star-Gazette*, shouted, There She Goes!

Townspeople remember a girl who used to love climbing Harris Hill in order to watch gliders soar over the farmlands in the Chemung River Valley. She was only six years old when the first woman went into space. She waited on tables in a pizza place while attending community college and saved her money until she had enough for 30 hours of lessons in single-engine planes at the age of 19. She picked up flying quickly, which was no surprise to her chemistry teacher at Elmira Free Academy where she had attended high school. Eileen was a determined young woman.

Eileen transferred to Syracuse University, where she graduated from college with a degree in mathematics and economics. Knowing that flying had to be part of her life, she joined the US Air Force, where she met and married fellow pilot Pat Youngs. She later earned a master of science degree in operations from Stanford University and a master of arts degree in space systems managements from Webster University.

After graduating from air force pilot training, she worked first as a T-38 instructor pilot and later as a C-141 instructor. Further study at the Air Force Institute of Technology led to an assignment at the US Air Force Academy as a mathematics professor and T-41 instructor pilot. She was awarded many medals for service and flying, including the Distinguished Flying Cross and the Defense Meritorious Service Medal. Before her retirement, she logged 6,751 flight hours in more than 30 types of aircraft.

Eileen was the second female accepted for air force test pilot training in 1979. While attending Air Force Test Pilot School at Edwards Air Force Base in California, Eileen was selected as an astronaut candidate, becoming an astronaut in 1991. She had several assignments at NASA before her first flight. Requirements for pilots were more stringent than those for mission specialists. A bachelor of science degree in engineering, physical science, or math was required. Candidates had to have at least 1,000 command pilot hours and 2,000 hours of experience in high-performance aircraft, such as flight testing. Pilots had to stand between five foot four and six foot four and have visual acuity of 20/70 correctable to 20/20.

Eileen met these requirements and was given the assignment to pilot *Discovery*. Her first challenge came soon after reaching orbit: the *Discovery* crew learned that one of the maneuver jets was stuck in a closed position and another had a small leak. The 42 other jets were working, so NASA gave the go ahead for the *Discovery* to rendezvous with *Mir*.

During *Discovery*'s eight-day mission, more than 20 scientific experiments were performed in a lab known as Spacelab onboard the shuttle. In one, wheat seedlings would be grown. NASA hoped that plants would be able to serve as a source of food in the future and also help to purify the air.

The *Discovery* also began a process to allow NASA to track and better understand space debris. Deploying and recovering a 2,600-pound satellite and testing new spacesuits in a spacewalk were all part of their assignments. Traveling more than 2.9 million miles in 198 hours and 29 minutes, Eileen's first trip into space as a pilot and second in command was a success. No one who knew her was surprised.

Eileen made her second journey into space, again as a pilot, on Mission STS-84 in 1997. Flying the *Atlantis*, the crew docked with the Russian space station where they transferred nearly four tons of equipment and supplies. This was the sixth shuttle mission to dock with *Mir*. It was time to start construction on the International Space Station.

Eileen made history again as the first female shuttle commander on *Columbia*'s STS-93 mission when the shuttle launched on a hot and humid day in July 1999. It was the 30th anniversary of the first Apollo moon landing. As commander, she was in charge of the shuttle and her four crewmates.

The launch began soon after midnight. People in the bleachers could hear a man counting back from 10. "10 . . . 9 . . . 8 . . . 7 . . . 6 . . . ," and he stopped. The sensor had shown a hydrogen leak in the engine. After the crew left the ship, it was checked out. There was no leak—just a faulty sensor. However, anytime a launch is started and stopped, it has to be postponed for 48 hours in order to restart the rockets.

Launch number two was also postponed, this time due to an electrical storm. But the third time was the charm; the *Columbia* space shuttle and its rocket boosters lit up the sky at 1 AM on July 23. But Eileen soon realized that all was not well. The liquid oxygen post pin came flying out of the main injector during the main engine ignition, puncturing three liquid hydrogen tubes.

Spacecraft need a combination of hydrogen and oxygen to reach a high enough altitude. The *Columbia* didn't have enough hydrogen now, and they were seven miles short of the target altitude. Eileen stayed calm, ordering several burns of the orbiter. Each burn led the *Columbia* closer to its target. Finally, they reached orbit with the largest payload to date—the *Chandra* X-ray Observatory. This telescope would allow astronomers to study black holes, exploding stars, and other phenomena in space. The 57-foot observatory weighed more than 20 tons. Deployment was a success. Hundreds of scientists on Earth would be able to gather data about the universe from the past 10 billion years.

The shuttle commander is the crew member who flies the shuttle during rendezvous and when the shuttle returns to Earth. Toward the end of this particular mission, the shuttle was supposed to grab a satellite. NASA wanted it done within a certain amount of time and with no more than four bursts of the shuttle jets. Eileen did it with just two.

The *Columbia* landing was particularly difficult. It was scheduled to be a night landing at Kennedy Space Center. Night landings were generally avoided because pilots don't have the visual cues and landmarks that they rely on during a day landing. Additionally, many landings were diverted to Edwards Air Force Base when bad weather occurred in the area. However, Eileen landed the *Columbia* on Runway 33 at Kennedy on July 27, 1999, at 11:20 PM.

Four years later, she was at home in Houston with her children when she carried her young son downstairs and turned on the television to check on the latest *Columbia* flight. Eileen was shocked to find that the shuttle had exploded upon returning to Earth. As the former chief of the Astronaut Safety Branch, she quickly volunteered to serve on the investigation team, but she was turned down because she already had a job. Eileen was on the schedule as shuttle commander for the next launch a month later.

Eileen had been training with her crew of three astronauts for a year. In addition to normal shuttle duties, they were to deliver three astronauts to the International Space Station and make repairs. The March launch of STS-114 was delayed while NASA and an investigation team that included Sally Ride tried to figure out what had happened with the *Columbia*—and keep it from happening again.

Knowing all seven astronauts who were killed in the *Columbia* disaster, Eileen suspended training for the first week. Two of her crew were assigned to support the families of those astronauts. The following week, she and the fourth crew member would continue with training.

More than three years later, STS-114 *Discovery* was finally ready to launch. It would be the first shuttle launch since the *Columbia*, and disaster was on everyone's mind. Reporters clamored to find out whether Eileen and the crew were worried. Eileen assured everyone that they were ready to fly as soon as

NASA said the shuttle was ready. "I believe in human exploration. I believe we need to go into Earth's orbit. We need to go
back to the moon and build a space station."

Two months before the rescheduled launch, Eileen was at
Johnson Space Center working on a simulated landing when the
altimeter gave a faulty reading. In light of all of the concerns about
the spaceflight, the faulty reading was scary. "That was a brand-
new one," Eileen said before finishing the landing sequence.[1]

Eileen's biggest challenge was talking to her daughter. At
seven years old, her daughter was old enough to hear things
about the dangers of spaceflight due to the destruction of the
Columbia shuttle. Eileen assured her daughter that she wouldn't
fly if it was unsafe.

Eileen's calm personality also reassured her crew. Before she
had even become an astronaut or had kids of her own, Eileen's
nickname was Mom. The nickname points to her leadership abilities; she makes the hard decisions and takes care of her people.

Mission STS-114 was called the "Return to Flight" mission.
Not only would they be remembering *Columbia*, but they also
would be testing shuttle safety. The future of the space program
depended upon the success of the mission. As a result of taking
every precaution, there were several delays.

At 10:39 AM on June 26, STS-114 *Discovery* launched from Kennedy Space Center. Although the launch was a success, officials
worried about falling debris during liftoff, even though a certain
amount of debris is normal. They learned that one of the objects
measured just an inch and a half long and came off an insulating
tile over the landing gear door. The shuttle also hit a bird.

The *Discovery* was scheduled to deliver supplies and make
repairs to the International Space Station. But first Eileen took
the shuttle under the space station and made a Rendevous Pitch
Maneuver in which she slowly flipped the shuttle end over end

while the ISS crew photographed the underside of the ship and the heat-resistant tiles. Eileen was the first pilot to perform this maneuver with a space shuttle.

After docking with the ISS, the crew made repairs, including replacing a broken gyroscope. They also tested safety and repair techniques, including how to repair damage to insulating tiles and panels.

As with most shuttle flights, the plan was to land the shuttle at Kennedy Space Center. NASA had tested more than 1,200 paths that the *Discovery* could take, but unpredictable weather made a Florida landing impossible.

"How do you feel about a beautiful, clear night with a breeze down the runway in the high desert of California?" asked Ken Ham at Mission Control.

"We are ready for whatever we need to do," Eileen answered.

As Eileen took the *Discovery* out of orbit and reentered the Earth's atmosphere at 25 times the speed of sound, pilot Colonel Kelly watched the controls for any signs of trouble. The spacecraft zoomed north of Los Angeles. People at Edwards Air Force Base heard a double sonic boom. Eileen landed the *Discovery* in the Mojave Desert in the early morning hours as people cheered at Mission Control.

STS-114 *Discovery* was called a success, yet NASA knew there was still a lot of work to do. Too many questionable situations had arisen before the launch, including problems with sensors. The foam from the shuttle fuel tank that was believed to have caused the explosion of the *Columbia* hadn't been resolved, either. Five large pieces of foam came off the *Discovery* tank but luckily did not cause the same problems.

The following year—after 36 days, 8 hours, and 10 minutes in spac—Colonel Eileen Collins retired from NASA as the first woman to pilot and command a space shuttle.

LEARN MORE

"Eileen Collins." NASA. http://starchild.gsfc.nasa.gov/docs/StarChild/whos_who_level2/collins.html.

"Eileen Collins—NASA's First Female Shuttle Commander to Lead Next Shuttle Mission." NASA. http://www.nasa.gov/news/highlights/Eileen_Collins.html.

Extraordinary Explorers and Adventurers by Judy Alter (Children's Press, 2000).

Onboard the Space Shuttle by Ray Spangenburg and Kit Moser (Franklin Watts, 2002).

CATHERINE "CADY" COLEMAN

....

MUSICAL ASTRONAUT

When Sally Ride became the first American woman in space, she inspired countless women. The number of women going into traditionally male fields like science and engineering began to increase. One of those women was Catherine Coleman, better known as Cady, an MIT student on the school crew team who was working on a bachelor's degree in chemistry when she met Sally Ride.

Cady had never considered being an astronaut before meeting the first American woman in space, but she began thinking about it as she enlisted in the air force. She had grown up in a

Expedition 26 flight engineer **Catherine "Cady" Coleman** at the International Space Station. *NASA*

military family, so joining the military made sense. Flying jets and exploring space also fit with her goals.

Assigned to Wright-Patterson Air Force Base as a second lieutenant, Cady worked as a research chemist. She created model compounds for use on advanced computers. While at Wright-Patterson, she also volunteered for medical trials for NASA at their aeromedical laboratory. This was where aviator Ruth Nichols had undergone astronaut testing, including the centrifuge, in the late 1950s. Cady was one of five women in the 20-person test group. She recalled that those women often outperformed the men. She set several endurance records herself.

Back at school, Cady earned her PhD in polymer science and engineering. A year later, she was selected for the astronaut program. Cady worked in many capacities at NASA. Like many before and after her, she served as capcom for both the shuttle and the International Space Station (ISS). She worked on the tile repair team for the "Return to Flight" shuttle commanded by Colonel Eileen Collins. Cady also served as chief of robotics. Her job was training astronauts in robotics. She was also the lead astronaut for long-term habitability on the ISS, a role that would serve her well in the coming years.

Cady got her chance to go to space as a mission specialist for STS-73 on the *Columbia* space shuttle. The flight was postponed six times before finally taking off on October 20, 1995. Two postponements were due to weather; the other four were due to mechanical problems. The delays were critical for the 16-day scientific mission with the second Microgravity Laboratory, a 22,000-pound pressurized laboratory, in the payload bay. A number of experiments using biotechnology, combustion science, and the physics of fluid would assist in studying the effects of weightlessness in space. In order to provide the most stability for the experiments, the *Columbia* was flown with its tail toward Earth.

Food in Space

In the early days of spaceflight, astronauts often dined on bite-sized cubes of food or on food squeezed out of tubes. Commercials in the early 1960s proclaimed that Tang was the drink of astronauts. The orange powder mixed with water had actually been around for a few years when the space program adopted it to improve the taste of water on the space capsules.

Fast-forward to the 21st century, and the typical diet is freeze-dried. What has changed is the packaging, which offers a lot more food choices. A special meal tray holds down containers of food, but astronauts have to finish one food container before they open another or their food might float off. After adding hot water, astronauts have a meal. With microgravity in spacecraft, liquids appear as droplets floating in the air. Drinking from pouches with straws is recommended.

But that's not all. Astronauts in space eat a lot of the same food that you do—peanut butter sandwiches, nuts, fruit, tortillas, cookies, and candy. And although you can't have pizza delivered, chocolate-vanilla swirl ice cream was included among the other supplies for the ISS crew in the summer of 2012. The crew decided to have a party.

This mission was practice for staying and working on the new International Space Station. The flight included Cady and four other new astronauts. Except for the pilot, the other four were scientists. Only the commander, Kenneth Bowersox, and payload commander Kathryn Thornton had flown before.

Chandra X-ray Observatory

Did you know that scientists can see into the past up to 10 billion years ago? No magic is involved—just a specially designed telescope that can pick up X-ray emissions from around the galaxy. These X-rays were emitted billions of years ago, but because they were so far away, they are just now reaching the earth. The data from these hot spots in the universe go to the Smithsonian Astrophysical Observatory at Harvard University. The observatory processes it and distributes the information to scientists around the world.

The most amazing telescope in the world was launched by the space shuttle *Columbia*, piloted by Eileen Collins, on January 23, 1999. It is traveling in an elliptical orbit high above the Earth. Most recently, it picked up X-rays from a supermassive black hole 12.4 billion light-years away. You can find out what *Chandra* is up to by going to http://chandra.harvard.edu/.

Cady, an astronomer, served as backup crew for several missions before being assigned her second spaceflight. She was the lead mission specialist for STS-93 *Columbia*, flying with Commander Eileen Collins. This important mission deployed the *Chandra* X-ray Observatory. Cady's skills were needed to deploy the telescope that would receive X-ray images of astronomical phenomena that was invisible to the human eye—galaxies millions of miles away.

Cady's third mission to space was as a flight engineer on the Russian *Soyuz* TMA-20 spacecraft. As part of Expedition 26, she and the rest of the crew launched from Baikonur, Russia, on

December 16, 2010. Their destination was the ISS, where Cady spent 159 days performing experiments and space station maintenance. As the lead robotics science officer, she used the robotic arm to capture *Kounotori*, a Japanese supply ship. It was the second robotic capture from the ISS.

An accomplished flutist, Cady became the space half of the first Earth-space musical duet a few months later. She and musician Ian Anderson (of Jethro Tull) played a flute duet in honor of the 50th anniversary of Yuri Gagarin's first flight into space.

Cady returned to Earth on Expedition 27, more than five months later, landing in Kazakhstan. In total, she has spent 4,330 hours in space.

A retired Air Force colonel, Cady continues as an active astronaut with NASA.

LEARN MORE

"Astronaut Cady Coleman Shares Her Love of the Flute from Space." NASA. www.nasa.gov/mission_pages /station/expeditions/expedition26/flute_on_iss.html.

"Meet Cady Coleman, Astronaut Mom" by Kim Segal and John Zarrella. CNN. http://articles.cnn.com/2009 -11-12/tech/cady.astronaut.mom_1_space-station-space -shuttle-columbia-johnson-space-center?_s=PM:TECH.

"Preflight Interview: Catherine Coleman." NASA. www.nasa.gov/mission_pages/station/expeditions /expedition26/coleman_interview.html.

PAMELA MELROY

PILOTING IN SPACE

Three heat-resistant panels on the *Discovery* space shuttle need replacing, said engineers at NASA's Engineering and Safety Center in 2007.[1] If the panels were not replaced, NASA might be looking at another disaster like the *Challenger* in 1986 or the *Columbia* in 2003.

NASA administrators in charge of the final decision about the launch disagreed, stating they had done everything possible to make the *Discovery* safe and that the level of risk was in the acceptable range. And there had been too many delays already. The International Space Station needed work, and two new lab-

Astronaut and pilot **Pamela Melroy** in an emergency bailout exercise as part of training before a flight to the International Space Station. *NASA*

oratories from Europe and Japan were ready to be joined to the space station.

John Logsdon, director of the Space Policy Institute at George Washington University and a member of the *Columbia* disaster investigation team, believed NASA was feeling scheduling pressure. A Florida newspaper said that NASA was rolling the dice in a risk that could cost the lives of more astronauts. Others said NASA was pushing for the launch because they feared budget cuts were coming from Congress.

NASA met with Pamela Melroy, a retired air force colonel and *Discovery* shuttle commander, and her crew of six. After a 12-hour discussion, the *Discovery* crew reported they were satisfied with the safety of their space shuttle. For Pam—an air force pilot with more than 5,000 flight hours on more than 45 different types of aircraft—being a pilot is just a rock-solid deep part of her identity.[2]

Pam, who was born in California but grew up in New York, was always interested in space. With a bachelor's degree in physics and astronomy from Wellesley College, she received a master of science degree in earth and planetary science from MIT a year later. She entered the air force through the ROTC program and received her initial pilot training at Reese Air Force Base in Lubbock, Texas. She flew the KC-10 and taught flying before going into combat. She flew more than 200 combat and combat support hours in Operation Desert Shield/Desert Storm in the Middle East and in Operation Just Cause in Panama.

Afterward, Pam attended the Air Force Test Pilot School at Edwards Air Force Base. She served as a test pilot for the C-17 Combined Test Force until her selection as a candidate for the astronaut program in 1994. For her flying skills, she was recognized with a number of awards: Air Force Meritorious Service Medal, First Oak Leaf Cluster; Air Medal, First Oak Leaf Cluster; Aerial Achievement Medal, First Oak Leaf Cluster; and the Expeditionary Medal, First Oak Leaf Cluster.

Pam was part of the astronaut class of 1995, and within a year she qualified as a shuttle pilot. On the ground, her first NASA duties included astronaut support for launches and landings. She also served as lead for the crew module of the *Columbia* Reconstruction Project Team and deputy project manager for the *Columbia* Crew Survival Investigation Team.

The 2007 *Discovery* flight to the ISS wasn't the first or even second time that Pam had flown to the ISS. She had served as pilot for STS-92 *Discovery* in 2000 and STS-112 *Atlantis* in 2002. On both flights, she was part of crews that installed pieces of the truss that would allow the space station to expand.

The STS-92 *Discovery*, the 100th space shuttle flight, hauled a nine-ton framework and a three-ton docking port when it launched. The framework, also known as the first truss, included four giant gyroscopes that would expand maneuverability of the station and equipment that would improve voice and visual transmission. It took four spacewalks, each lasting about six and a half hours, to connect the truss and the docking station. After 202 orbits around Earth, that first flight made the ISS ready for its first crew.

The space shuttles were grounded for three months in 2002 due to cracks in the fuel systems that needed to be repaired. But on October 7, the *Atlantis* launched for STS-112 with Pam serving as pilot again. The shuttle carried another piece of the truss, a 14-ton support beam for the space station that measured 45 feet long and 15 feet wide and carried a large part of the communications equipment for the space station. According to William Gerstenmaier, the Johnson Space Center space station program manager, the truss was basically a spacecraft that lacked its own propulsion. That propulsion was provided by the *Atlantis*.

In Mission STS-112 the *Atlantis* was the first shuttle that could be seen going from launching pad to orbit on television, thanks to a camera mounted on one of the external fuel tanks. This camera would also help Mission Control spot anything on the shuttle that needed attention. Both the external fuel tank and the camera were later jettisoned and left to burn up in the atmosphere once the fuel tank was empty.

Upon arrival at the space station, Pam and the *Atlantis* crew were greeted by a three-person crew—two Russian cosmonauts and American astronaut Dr. Peggy A. Whitson. As with previous flights, the station's robotic arm moved the large piece of equipment in place, but astronauts would have to take spacewalks to complete the attachment and connect the cables and wiring. Today, the electrical system of the ISS involves eight miles of electrical wiring. Pam assisted by serving as internal spacewalk choreographer for the three spacewalks.

On the third flight, as the second female shuttle commander after Eileen Collins, Pam would bring more modules to the space station. With the *Harmony* module they carried, the ISS would have even more capabilities for laboratories from various countries in the world. But many people had concerns about the *Discovery*'s safety.

On October 23, 2007, the STS-120 *Discovery* launched from Kennedy Space Center. As shuttle commander, Pam took over the controls as they neared the space station. She maneuvered through a difficult back flip of the huge *Discovery* about 600 feet from the station. This allowed the space station crew to photograph the belly of the shuttle to transmit to Mission Control.

Once the photography was complete, Pam turned the shuttle back over and docked with the space station at 8:40 AM. She revisited with Peggy, an old friend she had shared a previous mission with, who was now commander of the space station.

The two commanders had smiles and hugs for each other. By the end of the first day, Pam received a transmission from Mission Control. After studying the pictures that were sent back, they concluded that all looked well for the *Discovery*.

With that out of the way, the *Discovery* crew got to work installing modules and moving the 35,000-pound solar array and truss from the top of the station to the left end of the station. Things didn't always go as expected, though. For example, panels of the P6 Solar Array were damaged as they were moved. An unscheduled spacewalk had to be performed to repair the panels. With a lot of construction duties, plus these unexpected problems, the crews worked around the clock.

Two weeks later on Earth, people looked for a white dot moving quickly in the sky. It was the *Discovery* space shuttle zooming over North America. Those who didn't see it in the midday sun might have heard its double sonic boom. Soon after 1 PM, the *Discovery* touched down on a 15,000-foot landing strip at Kennedy Space Center with a happy Mission Control and an even happier *Discovery* crew. Mission STS-120 was a success; it was the kind of mission that made being an astronaut such an amazing job.

Pam Melroy later served as branch chief for the Orion branch of the Astronaut Office. Talk of ending the shuttle program began, and knowing that competition would be fierce to fly one of NASA's remaining shuttle flights, Pam decided to retire in 2009.

She moved to the Federal Aviation Administration as director of field operations for the Office of Commercial Space Transportation. But Colonel Pamela Melroy would always remember that being in space was like being someplace magical.[3]

LEARN MORE

Pamela Melroy Oral History. NASA. www.jsc.nasa.gov /history/oral_histories/MelroyPA/melroypa.htm.

"Preflight Interview: Pamela Melroy." NASA. www.nasa .gov/mission_pages/shuttle/shuttlemissions/sts120 /sts120_interview_melroy_prt.htm.

Women Astronauts by Laura S. Woodmansee (Collector's Guide Publishing, 2002).

PEGGY WHITSON

· · · · · · · · · · · · · · ·

SPACE STATION COMMANDER

Peggy Whitson has what it takes to be a leader. Part of her record 377 days in space was spent as the first female commander of the International Space Station. Afterward, she became the first woman to serve as chief of the Astronaut Office, essentially the head boss of all the astronauts on ground and in space.

Not bad for a girl from an Iowa hog and soybean farm. Her hometown, Beaconsfield, has a post office and a church. The population was 32. What made her decide to become an astronaut? At age nine, she watched Neil Armstrong and Buzz Aldrin walk on the moon, and she wanted to go to space, too. It didn't

Shuttle commander Pamela Melroy (left) greets International Space Station commander **Peggy Whitson** (right). *NASA* matter that there weren't any women astronauts at the time or that she hadn't heard of the Mercury 13.

Her father cemented her aspirations when he took her flying the next year over Iowa cornfields. Finally, when she was a senior in high school, she heard that NASA had selected their first women astronauts. Peggy knew being an astronaut was possible because of Shannon Lucid.[1]

Other people have dreams of becoming astronauts, too, but sometimes they give up. Peggy's self-proclaimed hardheaded determination kept her going, even when people tried to talk her out of it.[2] After earning a bachelor of science degree in biology and chemistry at Iowa Wesleyan College in three years, she moved to Houston to work on her doctorate in biochemistry even though two of her advisers urged her to go to medical school instead. But Houston was the home of Johnson Space Center, and she planned to work there some day.

In 1986, she got her foot in the door when Johnson Space Center hired her as a research biochemist; in this role, she planned space-oriented experiments. Later, she was appointed the deputy division chief of the Medical Sciences Division. And every year she applied for the astronaut program. In the 10th year, she was accepted. She never regretted her decision. "It's one of the only jobs I've had—flying in space—that I've got satisfaction from every day."[3]

Her first flight, as a flight engineer for Mission STS-111 on the *Endeavour* shuttle in 2002, was bound for the International Space Station (ISS) where she would spend six months as part of the Expedition 5 crew. The *Endeavour* not only carried the crew, but also brought important parts for the ISS robotic arm. The arm required a seven-hour "wrist surgery" to repair problems with the joints. Once it was repaired, Peggy used the arm to install two truss segments. She was also kept busy with jobs outside the shuttle, as well, such as installing shielding on a module during a space walk.

As the first science officer on the ISS, Peggy found the experiments they performed very fulfilling for their usefulness. The results would go somewhere.

It wasn't all work, though. She got to throw out the ceremonial first pitch of baseball's 2002 World Series. After six months in space, most people would be ready for home, but Peggy found leaving the station extremely difficult.[4]

Living with a lack of gravity was a challenge. In the lab, she had to get creative with her instruments, which would float off if she laid them down without attaching them to something. Using a bungee cord, she tied herself to the wall in order to sleep.

When she returned from her first mission, she trained at Star City in Russia as the backup ISS commander for Expedition 14, but it was Expedition 16 in 2007 that gave her the opportunity to be ISS commander. This time, however, she wouldn't be flying on a NASA space shuttle—she would fly on a Russian Soyuz spacecraft. Her crew included Russian cosmonaut Yuri Malenchenko and the first Malaysian astronaut, Dr. Sheikh Muszaphar Shukor.

Kent Rominger, chief of NASA's Astronaut Office, believed that Peggy was more than capable of running the ISS. "I think of Peggy as being gifted in everything—not only in space and life sciences, but also in operations, from robotics to spacewalking."[5]

The *Soyuz* TMA-11 launched from the Baikonur Cosmodrome in Kazakhstan on the morning of October 10, 2007, with Peggy on board. They reached orbit nine minutes later, and two days later they docked with the space station. While ISS commander, Peggy oversaw the first expansion of the ISS in six years. Solar wings were installed to provide electricity for two new science modules. Both working and living areas grew. By the time she left, the ISS was about the size of a football field.

The International Space Station

Imagine a football field. If your backyard is the size of a football field, you have a pretty big backyard. The largest manmade object in space is about the same size. It's the International Space Station or ISS, and it weighs more than 900,000 pounds.

Building started on the space station in 1998. Now complete, the ISS consists of different modules designated for research, service, and crew. The US laboratory is the *Destiny* module, although its experiments are meant to help everyone in the world. There is also a European laboratory, *Columbus,* and Japan contributed the *Kibo* (meaning "hope") module.

Large cylinders called nodes connect the modules to each other. Nodes aren't just connections, though. Astronauts use them for dining, recreation, and other purposes. There's even a gymnasium on board, since it's very important for astronauts to exercise while at the station. The *Quest* air lock is where the astronauts go when it's time for an EVA or a spacewalk. It's like a door to space.

With more than 125 launches to the station, it can be a busy place. Hundreds of people have visited, and it has been occupied continuously for more than 12 years.

Even as commander, Peggy had experiments to perform. In fact, she did 21. One experiment meant a lot to her on a personal level. The daughter of a soybean farmer, she grew soybeans in zero gravity. She kept her father informed about the progress of the plants, and the filtration system she tested has since been used on Earth for food preservation and in medicine.

Peggy also held the spacewalking record for a while. With six spacewalks to her credit, she has spent almost 40 hours, or the equivalent of the typical American workweek, walking in space. She said, "I think the important thing about records is that you need to keep breaking them and that we need to keep extending and going just a little bit further. . . . The records are only important as a marker for the next milestone that we're going to achieve more."[6]

Peggy and Malenchenko returned to Earth on the same Soyuz spacecraft a little more than six months later.

After 376 days, 17 hours, and 22 minutes in space, Peggy was ready for her next challenge. She didn't have to look far. She was appointed the first female chief of the Astronaut Office at NASA. She was the 12th astronaut to take on the position first held by Deke Slayton in 1962 for the first manned spaceflights. The chief of the Astronaut Office oversees everything about the astronauts, including training, assignments, and crew selection.

As challenging as the job normally was, it became even more so when NASA suffered several budget cuts. NASA's human spaceflight programs were canceled, and the space shuttles were retired. Instead, NASA would begin looking into hiring private companies to take people and supplies into space.

Flight opportunities for American astronauts dropped drastically, with only a handful of possibilities on Soyuz capsules. Part of Peggy's job was to choose the astronauts, a difficult task made more so by the changes in NASA, but publicly she announced, "We hope we will overcome this hurdle and continue to explore."[7]

Less than half the number of astronauts remained from a high of 150 in 2000. After serving in the Astronaut Office for three years, Peggy resigned in July 2012, but she would like to return to space some day. She hopes that NASA will eventually partner with a private company like SpaceX to send astronauts back to the ISS or even the moon.

LEARN MORE

"Commander Peggy Whitson's Space Station Journals." NASA.www.nasa.gov/mission_pages/station/expeditions /expedition16/journals_peggy_whitson.html.

"Preflight Interview: Peggy Whitson." NASA. www.nasa. gov/mission_pages/station/expeditions/expedition16 /exp16_interview_whitson.html.

Women Astronauts by Laura S. Woodmansee (Collector's Guide Publishing, 2002).

SUNITA WILLIAMS

• • • • • • • • • • • • • •

BREAKING RECORDS

People throughout America were starting to say good-bye to summer on September 5, 2012. Although the calendar wouldn't mark summer's end for a couple more weeks, the Labor Day holiday two days earlier had mentally prepared people for autumn and a new school year.

More than two hundred miles above Earth, astronaut Sunita Williams stepped, or rather floated, outside the International Space Station at 6:06 AM Central Standard Time. Sunita had arrived at the ISS on July 16 on a Soyuz spacecraft. This was her second long-term stay at the station. As a flight engineer for Expedition 32, Sunita and Japanese astronaut Akihiko Hoshide

Flight engineer **Sunita Williams** (left) and ISS commander Michael Lopez-Alegria (right) prepare for a spacewalk during Expedition 14. *NASA*

had been working on repairs to a spare power unit. Five days earlier, they had spent 8 hours and 17 minutes outside the station, just 39 minutes short of the record for the longest single spacewalk set in 2001 by astronauts Susan Helms and James Voss.

The earlier spacewalk, the fifth for Williams, a navy commander, had allowed her to connect one of two power cables needed for a Russian laboratory unit that would soon be arriving. The two astronauts also removed a failed power distributor. But problems driving the bolts into the replacement meant a return spacewalk was required. They also needed to replace a camera on the Canadarm2 robotic arm.

As 2 hours and 12 minutes passed into this sixth spacewalk, Sunita and Akihiko were still working on the power unit and far from done. Sunita's boss, chief of astronauts Peggy Whitson, sent Sunita a message via Mission Control. "It's an honor to hand off the record to someone as talented as you. You go, girl."[1]

Sunita had officially passed Peggy Whitson's spacewalking record for the most time spent on spacewalks by any woman in the world. After a brief moment of satisfaction, Sunita and Akihiko continued with their task. It was clear that damaged bolt threads were causing the problem with attaching the power distributor. Using a toothbrush, bristle tool, and compressed nitrogen gas guns, they cleaned metal shavings out of a threaded socket. They were then able to drive in the bolt. The power distributor was operational, and now seven out of eight power channels were powering the one-million-pound space station. The eighth one had short-circuited and would need to be replaced at some future time.

After replacing a camera assembly on the ISS robotic arm, Sunita reentered the space station almost 6½ hours later, for a total of 44 hours and 2 minutes of walking in space. She added to that on November 1 with a seventh spacewalk and now has spent 50 hours and 40 minutes walking in space. She touched down in Russia on November 18, 2012. She has spent 322 days in space since becoming an astronaut.

Sunita's first trip into space was for Expeditions 14 and 15 from 2006 to 2007, the 20th mission to the space station. Her trips occurred on American spacecraft, launching on the *Discovery* and returning on the *Atlantis*. As flight engineer at the station, she worked the ISS robotic arm and Special Purpose Dexterous Manipulator in addition to undertaking four EVAs.

There were many difficult tasks involved with adding a structural truss and reconfiguring the electrical system so that it would get power from the solar panels that had already been installed. The spacewalks, undertaken with Captain Michael Lopez-Alegria, meant carefully moving fluid lines filled with toxic ammonia coolant. Astronauts couldn't take any ammonia back inside or it would contaminate the station. Toxic ammonia can cause burning of the eyes, nose, and throat—and in high doses, death.

Sunita again had to tackle toxic ammonia coolant on her last spacewalk in November when a leak was spotted. She and fellow astronaut Akihiko left the ISS through the US *Quest* air lock and made their way to the far left side of the station's central truss to reroute coolant lines.

The solar arrays that power the station build up heat and are cooled with a thermal control system that sends the ammonia to radiators to take care of excessive heat. After exposure to the coolant, astronauts must go through a decontamination procedure before entering the station. Ammonia flakes are bushed off suits before the suits are left in direct sunlight to remove the remaining ammonia.

Ten days after breaking Whitson's record, Sunita took over as commander of the International Space Station, the second female commander in its history after Whitson. All of Sunita's training and time spent on the ISS prepared her for a challenge that she admitted to be being excited about.

According to Sunita, the ISS was at times as busy as a truck stop on the New Jersey Turnpike, with Japanese and Russian cargo ships coming and going, Russian spacecraft dropping off and picking up astronauts, and a private spacecraft called the *Dragon* arriving, as well.[2] Within a 17-day period, nine spacecraft docked with the ISS. Up to six people have resided on the ISS at one time.

Sunita and the international crew launched on July 14 from the Baikonur Cosmodrome in Kazakhstan, the same location that the first man in space, Yuri Gagarin, had launched from. When Sunita arrived at the ISS three days later, it was the 37th anniversary of the first American-Russian spacecraft docking.

The view from the ISS is nothing short of spectacular. Sunita reported seeing the many wildfires of summer 2012 in the United States, not to mention hurricanes like Ernesto and Isaac. The views of the hurricanes were much different than what she had experienced 20 years earlier as a naval officer in charge of Hurricane Andrew relief operations in Florida. But the view from space is one she never tires of.

The daughter of an Indian father and a Slovenian mother, Sunita is the second of both nationalities to be an astronaut. Her father, Dr. Deepak Pandya, is a well-known neuroanatomist. Sunita was born in Euclid, Ohio, but grew up in Needham, Massachusetts. Her parents still live in nearby Falmouth.

Sunita attended the US Naval Academy, earning an undergraduate degree in physical science and training as a naval aviator and diver. As a naval aviator, she received specialized helicopter training and was deployed to assist in the Gulf War and in Operation Provide Comfort to provide humanitarian aid afterward.

She later received a master of science in engineering management, attended test pilot training, and served as an instructor. A member of the Society of Experimental Test Pilots and the Society of Flight Test Engineers, she has logged more than 3,000 flight hours in more than 30 types of aircraft.

After acceptance into the astronaut program in 1998, Sunita's training expanded to include technical briefings, physiological training, water and wilderness survival instruction, and preparing for T-38 flight training. Before her journeys into space, she lived in the underwater Aquarius habitat for the NEEMO 2 mission for nine days.

When home, Sunita and her husband, Michael J. Williams, reside in Florida with an active Jack Russell terrier named Gorby and a Labrador retriever named Bailey. Sunita likes to stay active. Snowboarding and bow hunting are among her favorite activities. She really enjoys triathlons as well, and she hasn't let being in space keep her from participating.

NASA Goes Under Water

NASA isn't just about space; they also operate NASA Extreme Environment Mission Operations (NEEMO). Astronauts, scientists, and engineers travel to the depths of the ocean to Aquarius, a research station 62 feet below the water's surface. Aquarius is located 3.5 miles off Key Largo, Florida. It's believed that the ocean environment can help in training for space exploration. Under water, crew members are known as aquanauts instead of astronauts.

During her first stay at the ISS, she ran the Boston Marathon on April 16, 2007, on a treadmill. A bungee cord kept her from floating away. Her official time was 4 hours, 23 minutes, and 10 seconds. For her second stay, she decided to tackle California's Nautica Malibu Triathalon—swimming half a mile, biking 18 miles, and running 4 miles. As one of 5,000 athletes in the event, her participation was definitely the most unique. Her partner was Dr. Sanjay Gupta, a CNN medical correspondent, who did his triathlon on Earth. While he swam in the Pacific Ocean, she did the equivalent in bench presses on a specially designed weight machine called the Advanced Resistive Exercise Device (ARED). Gupta moved to biking and then running through Malibu while Sunita biked on a stationary bicycle and ran on a treadmill at the space station.

The ISS stationary bicycle has pedals but no seat. A computer controls the resistances and speed while tracking the heart rate. For the hills, she increased the resistance to match the route that people on Earth were taking.

Sunita had to use a harness with the treadmill to keep from floating off. While the lack of gravity might make a triathlon sound easier, it's not. When you simulate gravity—whether you're on the treadmill or the ARED—it sort of hurts. So it was a bit of an adjustment to get into the exercise.[3]

Sunita once again proved that there's nothing you can't do in space!

LEARN MORE

Astronaut Sunita Williams Achiever Extraordinaire by Capt. S. Seshadri and Aradhika Sharma (Rupa & Co., 2007).

"Flight Engineer Sunita Williams' Space Station Journals." NASA.www.nasa.gov/mission_pages/station/expeditions /expedition15/journals_sunita_williams.html.

"Sunita Williams' Frequently Asked Questions." NASA. www.nasa.gov/mission_pages/station/expeditions /expedition15/Williams_FAQ_7.html.

BARBARA MORGAN

....

TEACHERS IN SPACE

Barbara Morgan breathed a sigh of relief as the *Endeavour* reached Earth's orbit. Like all astronauts, she knew that the most dangerous part of spaceflight wasn't actually being in space but lifting off and returning to Earth. With delight, she looked out the *Endeavour*'s window at the beautiful Earth below. After almost 22 years, she had finally made it. Barbara Morgan became the first teacher in space on August 8, 2007.

"Morgan is racing toward space on the wings of a legacy," said the launching announcer on the ground.[1] The *Endeavour* was on its way to the International Space Station to deliver sup-

---

Barbara Morgan (left) and Christa McAuliffe (right) were the backup and primary candidates for the Teacher in Space Program. *NASA*

plies, add another section to the station backbone, and test a system of transferring electrical power to the shuttle.

As a mission specialist—or as she called it, an "educator mission specialist"—Barbara was busy. She operated the shuttle's robotic arm, even transferring supplies to the space station's robotic arm. NASA made it clear that Barbara was an astronaut first, but Barbara made it clear that she approached her duties with the mind, eyes, ears, and heart of a teacher.[2]

Because of her busy schedule, Barbara was only allowed six hours for education purposes, although she would be teaching quite a bit about the experience once she returned to Earth. On day seven, she interacted with students at the Discovery Center of Idaho through video. The next day, she spoke to students at the Challenger Center, founded by the wife of the *Challenger* commander, June Scobee Rodgers. The rest of education time was spent making videos of "teachable moments."

Spaceflights almost always include experiments, and this one was no different. Barbara had 10 million seeds of basil, an herb. When she returned, they would be distributed to students all over the US to grow in growth chambers they had designed. She would also use some lesson plans created by her friend Christa McAuliffe.

As with *Columbia*, a damaged tile was noted on the *Endeavour*. NASA studied pictures of the shuttle and decided it was not a danger. However, a hurricane on Earth meant leaving the space station a day early. Barbara's friends and family held their breath as the *Endeavour* reentered the atmosphere, clapping, hugging, and crying when it was successful.

In the early 1980s, NASA and the government had started batting around the idea of sending a private citizen into space on a space shuttle. Many professions were discussed, including journalists, who make their living writing about such things. But

President Ronald Reagan said that an educator should be first. In 1984, the Teacher in Space Program was launched because a teacher could have the greatest impact by teaching from space.

The first order of business was to choose a candidate. After the announcement, NASA received 10,463 applications. When Barbara heard about the opportunity, she shot straight up and said, "Wow!"[3] A dedicated teacher who had taught in South America and on a Native American reservation before teaching in a small Idaho town, Barbara believed in a hands-on approach to teaching.

Each state's candidates were narrowed down to two, which still left 100 candidates. Like all astronauts, the teachers underwent extensive medical and psychological testing, as well as interviews with committees and NASA officials. It wasn't just that a candidate had to be able to withstand the rigors of space-flight—a teacher-astronaut would be interacting with media and representing NASA at many events, as well.

NASA administrator James M. Beggs chose 10 finalists among the group. Six of the group were women; four were men. More tests, training, and interviews followed. The evaluation process was a full-time job.

Finally, NASA was ready to announce who would be the first teacher in space on July 19, 1985: Christa McAuliffe. Barbara was chosen as an alternate. She would train with the teacher-astronaut, and if for any reason the primary candidate was unable to fulfill the mission, the alternate would step in.

Christa McAuliffe, a social studies teacher from New Hampshire, was known for focusing on the experiences of ordinary people as much as the famous ones in her high school lessons for Concord High School. She even developed a course called "The American Woman" to teach about those experiences. On her application to NASA, she wrote, "I want to demystify NASA and

Christa McAuliffe tried out weightlessness on board NASA's KC-135 "zero gravity" aircraft. *NASA*

space flight. I want students to see and understand the special perspective of space and relate it to them."[4]

Like many of the early women astronauts, Christa witnessed the beginnings of space exploration from her family television in Framingham, the Boston suburb where she grew up. She communicated her excitement and fascination about space in interviews with NASA officials and in later interviews on talk shows and with reporters.

Right after the announcement, Christa promised that she would be "taking ten souls" with her as she and the other nine finalists had become very good friends. For five months, Christa and Barbara trained with the *Challenger* space shuttle crew. They practiced emergency landings, escapes, and putting out fires. Shuttle commander Dick Scobee made sure they knew the risks.

The first teacher in space would serve as a payload specialist on Mission STS-51L with six other astronauts, including the second American woman in space, Judith Resnik. Christa developed six lesson plans. She would be teaching from space and keeping a diary to humanize her experience and share it with others.

The *Challenger* launched from Kennedy Space Center on January 28, 1986. It had a larger-than-usual viewing audience due to Christa's presence. She had captured the hearts of Americans everywhere with her joy for teaching. Among the spectators were Christa's family, Barbara, and the other finalists of the program. Barbara was thrilled for her friend. As the rocket launched, Barbara bounced up and down and clapped. She yelled, "Bye, Christa. Bye, crew."[5]

Suddenly there was a loud boom, and plumes of smoke spiraled through the sky. Everyone looked at each other, asking what had happened. Those who could, including Barbara, ran toward the launch site. They soon learned that the *Challenger* had exploded, killing the crew. Barbara and the other finalists mourned the death of their good friend.

Barbara returned to teaching second and third grades in McCall, Idaho, a small town of 2,000 popular with tourists because of the mountains and Payette Lake at the north end of town. She continued working with NASA to promote space travel, telling all who would listen that America needed to push forward in space exploration. Barbara insisted that both she and Christa had known the risks they were taking. As a fellow finalist in the Teacher in Space Program said, Barbara became the voice of seven astronauts.

In 1998, Barbara was called to service again. With some regret over the prospect of leaving her students, Barbara finished the school year before she began training again. NASA was ready for a teacher in space, although the Teacher in Space Program had been discontinued. Barbara would train like any other astronaut. She was one of 31 astronauts in the 1998 class, along with Sunita Williams.

In 2002, she was assigned to Mission STS-118 on the *Columbia* shuttle, scheduled for a November 2003 launch. Yet nine months before her flight, the *Columbia* exploded upon reentry. The shuttle program was grounded until NASA could make sure it wouldn't happen again.

Barbara's flight was delayed until August 2007; it would be the 20th flight of the *Endeavour*, a shuttle named by school children in the United States after the *Challenger* disaster. Many finalists and semifinalists from the Teacher in Space Program attended her launch. Another spectator was Mercury 13 astronaut Gene Nora (Stumbough) Jessen, another friend of Barbara's.

As the sole survivor of the crew that had trained for the *Challenger*, Barbara took the memories of the *Challenger* crew with her on the flight to the space station in addition to mementos connected to Christa McAuliffe. One of the members of her new crew was Tracy Caldwell, who was inspired to become an astronaut by Christa.

Barbara had been waiting for this moment for almost half of her life. She traveled 5.3 million miles in 12 days, 17 hours, 55 minutes, and 34 seconds. For the next four months, she gave interviews, spoke at events, and met with students.

A year after her flight, Barbara retired from NASA and became the distinguished educator in residence at Boise State University. She insists that she's not a celebrity; she is and always will be a teacher.

Barbara Morgan isn't the only teacher-astronaut now. Dorothy Metcalf-Lindenburger is another. The daughter of two teachers, Dorothy, often called Dottie, taught earth science and astronomy in Washington State. In fact, it was while teaching her students about space that she found a website with applications for those interested in becoming educator astronauts. She applied and was chosen for astronaut training in February 2006. Dorothy went to space as a mission specialist on Mission STS-131 *Discovery* in 2010. She also flew to the International Space Station.

LEARN MORE

A Journal for Christa: Christa McAuliffe, Teacher in Space by Grace George Corrigan (University of Nebraska Press, 2000).

"Barbara Morgan Talks with Students on Ham Radio." NASA. www.nasa.gov/multimedia/podcasting/STS118 _morgan_radio.html.

Christa McAuliffe: A Space Biography by Laura S. Jeffrey (Enslow, 1998).

"In Their Own Words: Barbara Morgan." NASA. www .nasa.gov/multimedia/podcasting/morgan_itow.html.

"Preflight Interview: Barbara Morgan." NASA. www .nasa.gov/mission_pages/shuttle/shuttlemissions /sts118/morgan_interview.html.

. . . .

PART IV

WORLD ASTRONAUTS

American women weren't the only women not being taken seriously in the space industry. Women in other parts of the world were also barred from participating, or at least discouraged from doing so. Some still are. Many women in other parts of the world haven't had the opportunities that American women have had to pursue careers as astronauts—until recently.

Many developed countries have space agencies for the research and study of space. As of 2012, only three countries have had direct experience with manned spaceflight: the United States, Russia, and China. Although China started much later than the United States and Russia, they have already sent their first female astronaut into space.

In some cases, it's not a matter of technology but cost. It takes money and resources to launch a space program. Alone, countries like France, Italy, and Great Britain might find themselves limited. But by pooling resources, they created the European Space Agency, a 20-country organization that continues to grow and develop.

After World War II, many of the scientific minds that focused on rocket and space research moved to the United States or the Soviet Union, but not all scientists relocated. Some remained in their home countries, and in the late 1950s and early '60s, they also experimented with rocket-fueled flight. Fifty years ago, Norway launched its first rocket from its Andoya rocket range. Since then, more than a thousand rockets have been launched.

By 1960, scientists from 10 European countries formed a space research group known as GEERS. (GEERS is an acronym for *Groupe d'etudes europeen pour la collaboration dans le domaine des recherches spatiales*, which roughly translated from French means "European group studies for collaboration in the field of space research.") It fueled the European Launcher Development Organisation (ELDO), started in the early 1960s by six countries—France, Germany, the United Kingdom, Italy, Belgium, and Australia. Its primary focus was launch systems. A couple of years later, the European Space Research Organisation (ESRO) was created for space research.

Over the next several years, however, grumblings within the agencies arose, and ELDO disbanded. ESRO evolved into the European Space Agency (ESA) by 1975 to encompass the goals of both previous agencies. Other countries joined as well.

ESA worked out an agreement with NASA to build a science lab for space. *Spacelab* would be part of space shuttle flights. ESRO provided the modules in exchange for having European astronauts fly on the space shuttle. Ulf Merbold of Germany was the first ESA astronaut to fly on the shuttle for the STS-9 *Spacelab* mission, the first of 25 *Spacelab* flights until construction started on the International Space Station.

The ESA remains involved in space research. Efforts to have an operational next-generation launcher by 2020 is one of the agency's goals. Another is more political—merging the economic-based membership of the European Union with the science-directed European Space Agency.

Progress for women astronauts didn't proceed quite as quickly. It wasn't until 1991 that a woman from a country other than the United States or Russia went into space. She was British chemist Helen Sharman, who had been employed at a candy factory. One day she heard an advertisement on the car radio that caught her attention: "Astronaut wanted. No experience necessary."[1]

The ad was part of a Soviet promotion to take people into space. Essentially, they were selling a seat on Russian spaceflights to astronauts from other countries. They had already taken people from Japan, Cuba, Austria, Syria, Afghanistan, and Mongolia to space—at a price.

Helen Sharman was chosen from more than 13,000 applicants. She almost didn't get to go when the British government refused to fund her flight. Private funding through Project Juno saved the day.

After training at Star City for 18 months, she could speak Russian and was prepared for space travel. She flew as a research cosmonaut on *Soyuz* TM-12 to the *Mir* Space Station. She spent eight days in space performing agricultural experiments, such as seeing how pansies grew in zero gravity, but she never went into space again.

Anousheh Ansari is another woman who went into space as the first female commercial spaceflight participant. As a child, on summer nights in Iran, she would sleep on her grandparent's balcony and look at the stars, wondering what it would be like to be among them. Years later, she became the first person from Iran and the first Muslim to travel to space.

When Anousheh was 12 years old, a revolution started in Iran. Her school was shut down, and the environment became

Space Debris

• •

If you think of space as a gigantic area in which vast distances separate planets, you might be surprised, particularly if you're looking around the Earth. More than a half million pieces of space debris circle our planet. Where does it come from? Well, if you consider that countries have been sending things into orbit for more than 50 years, you might get an idea.

Some people call it space junk. Old spaceships and parts of spaceships, satellites, and other objects speed around the globe at 17,500 mph. Even a tiny object going at this speed can cause damage to spaceships and space stations.

The Department of Defense, along with NASA and other space agencies, track this space debris. In February 2009, an old Russian satellite collided with a working US satellite. Both satellites broke into thousands of pieces. NASA has guidelines on what to do to avoid collisions, sometimes known as "debris avoidance maneuvers," but they only know about objects that are larger than softballs. Sometimes the danger is too small to track. Paint flecks have caused enough damage to space shuttle windows that they've had to be replaced.

dangerous. She and her family immigrated to the United States. Today, she is an engineer and an American citizen. She traveled to space and the International Space Station on a Soyuz flight. She is often referred to as the first female space tourist because she rode on a commercial space mission.

Female astronauts are a lot like male astronauts. A dream begins often, but not always, in childhood. That dream to experience space is buried in some people. Others do whatever they can to make that dream come true. Here are some of those stories.

ROBERTA BONDAR

·············

LIVING A CHILDHOOD DREAM

Childhood dreams are important, and Roberta Bondar had a childhood dream of becoming an astronaut. "When I was eight years old, to be a spaceman was the most exciting thing I could imagine."[1]

Roberta realized her childhood dream when she took off on the 14th flight of the *Discovery* space shuttle on January 22, 1992. Not only was she Canada's first female astronaut, she was also the first non-American woman to fly on a US space shuttle.

As part of Mission STS-42, Roberta was a member of a seven-person crew on the *Discovery* that launched from Kennedy

Canadian astronaut **Roberta Bondar** gets into the Microgravity Vestibular Investigation (MVI) chair to begin an experiment in the International Microgravity Lab-1 (IML-1) science module. *NASA*

Space Center. She and Ulf Merbold, a German physicist who had first flown on a NASA space shuttle in 1983, were the payload specialists and part of the first international crews that would fly on space shuttles to prepare for doing similar work on the International Space Station when it was completed and ready for occupancy.

Mission STS-42 was also the most ambitious scientific mission to date, with 54 experiments related to materials research and life sciences. Experiments were coming from 16 different countries. The experiments represented the work of 200 scientists from around the world, with countries such as China having their first experiments on a space shuttle. In addition to experiments, the crew of STS-42 looked at making materials in space, such as crystals and alloys. This type of research could affect the creation of medicines in addition to electronics. Digital video, data, and communications between the *Discovery* crew and the Spacelab Mission Operations Control facility at the Marshall Space Center in Huntsville, Alabama, allowed more people to collaborate on experiments. Scientists on Earth could see the experiments, make adjustments, and receive data.

The *Discovery* would also be carrying 113 student experiments. But its largest payload was a pressurized laboratory installed in the payload bay more than a month before launch: the International Microgravity Laboratory (IML-1). The 23-foot-long, 13-foot-wide chamber was put to work as soon as the *Discovery* was in orbit 184 miles above Earth.

With only a week to perform experiments, the shuttle crew worked around the clock to complete as many experiments as possible. This meant working in 12-hour shifts. Roberta went to work by crawling through a 20-foot tunnel to reach the laboratory. The first hours were very important for activating the lab. Equipment had to be set up and turned on. Biological samples had to be quickly moved from crew-cabin lockers to the lab before they started to degrade. Living organisms that were to be used in experiments included fruit flies, worms, oat and wheat seedlings, blood cells, bacteria, and the eggs and sperm of African clawed frogs.

The laboratory is used to test the effects of reduced gravity on people and a host of other organisms. Because the extremely low levels of gravity—less than 1/1,000 the level on Earth—have an effect on organisms and materials, the *Discovery* minimized the shaking of the spacecraft by flying it with its tail pointed toward Earth. This "gravity-gradient stabilized" attitude used natural forces to maintain the shuttle in orbit and reduced the need to use stabilizing rockets that might disturb the ship and the experiments inside.

Some of the questions scientists hoped to answer were: How do wheat seedlings respond to different types of light in space? Are bacteria more resistant to antibiotics in space, and if so, why? What effect does gravity have on embryonic development? What are the effects of gravity on a variety of living organisms, including humans?

As the first neurologist in space, Roberta was conducting more than 40 experiments. She was particularly interested in how the human body adapted to low levels of gravity. She studied what the inner ear did when exposed to low gravity. Placing crew members in a chair that turned and twisted, she checked their eyes and responses. She would continue testing and evaluating the human body in space when she returned to Earth with data from 24 space missions. The results would provide NASA with information that would help in preparing astronauts for longer stays on the planned space station.

Back pain and tension were complaints for two-thirds of the people in space. Researchers already knew that the spine elongated up to almost three inches in limited gravity. Although being taller in space doesn't sound too bad, the back pain that came with it was. Roberta recorded the changes in spines during and after the flight.

Another "crew member" of *Discovery* was an IMAX camera, a large-format camera flown on several shuttle missions as a joint project of NASA, the National Air and Space Museum, and the IMAX Corporation. It provided views of space that few had seen.

By conserving on supplies, the STS-42 crew was able to squeeze an extra day into their trip. After eight days, they deactivated the lab, reentered Earth's atmosphere, and aimed the space shuttle toward Edwards Air Force Base in California. There wasn't any attempt to land at Kennedy Space Center due to the extra weight of the 23,201-pound IML. The extra weight affected the lift and drag of the flight, making it difficult to go the extra distance to Kennedy Space Center.

This was what Roberta had been working toward for years. Her parents had always encouraged Roberta and her sister to be goal oriented. Many of Roberta's goals were in the sciences, and her father built her a laboratory in their home's basement. Her high school science project led to a job at the Great Lakes Forestry Centre studying the spruce budworm. She received undergraduate degrees in zoology and agriculture, a graduate degree in experimental pathology, a doctorate in neurobiology, and a medical degree.

In 1983, NASA approached Canada about sending an astronaut on the space shuttle. The Canadian Space Agency (CSA) was born and soon called for applications to the program. After receiving more than 4,000 applications, the CSA chose six people to be in the first class of astronauts. One of those people was Roberta Bondar, who became the first Canadian woman and second Canadian in space. As of 2012, she is the first of only two Canadian women who have traveled to space. The other, Julie Payette, has been a member of two NASA missions and has logged 611 hours in space.

After being chosen as a Canadian astronaut, Roberta was appointed chairperson of the Canadian Life Sciences Subcommittee for Space Station the following year. After her spaceflight, she retired from the space agency to continue research. Two of her interests included the environment and the effects of reduced gravity on stroke patients. She has also pursued many interests, including flying, scuba diving, and photography. In addition to exhibiting and publishing books of her photography, she is also a highly sought speaker.

LEARN MORE

Maple Leaf in Space: Canada's Astronauts by John Melady (Dundurn, 2011).

"Roberta Bondar." NASA. www.nasa.gov/externalflash /the_shuttle/30.html.

Roberta Bondar website. www.robertabondar.com.

CHIAKI MUKAI

∙∙∙∙∙∙∙∙∙∙∙∙∙∙∙∙

OPENING DOORS

The second International Microgravity Laboratory (IML-2) flight came two years later as part of STS-65, the 17th *Columbia* mission. Even more ambitious than IML-1, the IML-2 contained 82 experiments, 31 more than IML-1.

The IML-2 mission shared many similarities with the first microgravity lab, specifically studying the effects of gravity on living things and various metals. It also included experiments from scientists from 13 countries around the world. However, it lasted five more days. According to NASA, STS-65 was a door opener for the space station.[1]

Payload specialist **Chiaki Mukai** squeezes hand cream from a tube and watches while it floats in zero gravity. *NASA*

Taking off at 12:43 PM on July 8, the *Columbia* space shuttle and crew spent the 25th anniversary of *Apollo 11* landing on the moon by continuing the exploration of space. A doctor, Chiaki Mukai from Japan, was a member of the international crew. Chiaki, from the Japan Aerospace Exploration Agency, was the first Japanese woman in space. During her first mission, she had investigated the autonomic nerve system, cardiovascular system, and bone and muscle metabolism.

Soon after reaching orbit, Chiaki and other crew members retreated to the bus-sized lab to set things up and activate the laboratory. Their equipment included thousands of animals, including various types of aquatic animals, fish, and Japanese red-bellied newts. After Germany and the United States, Japan contributed the largest number of experiments.

What intrigued Chiaki about space was how she would feel about gravity. The limited gravity, known as microgravity, affects the inner ear, eye, and touch. These are the senses that give us an idea of where our bodies are. As Chiaki had experienced limited gravity in simulated training environments, space didn't feel much different, although she admitted that when she was sent to space, she couldn't tell the ceiling from the floor.[2]

Reentering Earth's atmosphere and its gravity made the biggest impact. Her arms felt incredibly heavy, and for a few hours she kept testing objects like books and pencils to see how they behaved in gravity. She was amazed when they fell to the ground.

When Chiaki launched on her second flight with STS-95 *Discovery* in 1998, she became the first person from Japan to go into space twice. STS-95 wasn't primarily a medical research mission as her previous one had been. The crew also deployed the *Spartan* solar-observing spacecraft and the *Hubble* Space Telescope Orbital Systems Test Platform.

However, Chiaki was involved in a medical study that tried to measure the effects of spaceflight on aging. One of the subjects she studied on that spaceflight was former Mercury astronaut and US senator John Glenn. Glenn, who was the first American to orbit the Earth, was 77 years old when he flew on Mission STS-95. About Chiaki, he said, "She has more energy than anyone I know of."[3]

Aging in Space

··

When astronauts go into space, their muscles atrophy and they experience bone loss. For years, physicians have noted the same things in some of their patients. They are common signs of aging. On Earth, everything is pulled down because of gravity. The muscles, bones, and circulatory system all work against gravity to keep us upright.

When someone experiences the lack of gravity in space, body fluids shift and cause swelling in the face. Bones and muscles don't have to work against gravity, so they go unused. Muscles waste away, and bone mass diminishes. Exercise in space is very important to minimize bone loss, although people may lose some bone mass regardless.

The connection between space and aging could be important, so both gerontologists (people who study aging) and space medicine specialists plan on further study.

Born in Tatebayashi, in Japan's Gunma Prefecture, Chiaki came to NASA spaceflights with impressive medical credentials. After receiving her medical degree in 1977, she worked as a surgeon and later specialized in cardiovascular surgery. Chiaki was an assistant professor at the Department of Cardiovascular Surgery at Keio University in Japan. She also earned a doctorate in physiology, the study of living organisms.

In 1985, Japan's National Space Development Agency (NASDA), the precursor to the Japan Aerospace Exploration Agency, selected three people to train as payload specialists for the First Material Processing Test (FMPT) on the Spacelab mission. Chiaki was one of those three.

Chiaki began training with NASA in 1985 as a payload specialist, later serving as backup payload specialist for the final Spacelab mission. Although Chiaki didn't fly on that first mission, she did serve as Spacelab communicator for crew science operations. Additionally, her contributions to medical research in space have been invaluable. While awaiting her mission, she was appointed as a visiting scientist of the Division of Cardiovascular Physiology at the NASA Johnson Space Center. She later taught at the Baylor College of Medicine and became a visiting professor at the Keio University School of Medicine.

With more than 566 hours in space, Chiaki continued working for NASA as a deputy mission scientist, coordinating science operations for STS-107 *Columbia*. Her duties had ended by the time the *Columbia* reentered Earth's atmosphere and met its tragic end, as well.

She loves teaching and sharing what she knows of space and space medicine. She has been a visiting professor at the International Space University, as well.

In 2003, Japanese space agencies—NASDA, the Institute of Space and Astronautical Science (ISAS), and the National

Aerospace Laboratory of Japan (NAL)—merged and became the Japan Aerospace Exploration Agency (JAXA). Chiaki returned to Japan as senior adviser to the executive director of JAXA, Naoko Yamazaki.

Naoko Yamazaki was the second female astronaut from Japan. She assisted in developing the centrifuge for the International Space Station before becoming an astronaut. Naoko went through training in Japan, Russia, and the United States. She's a certified Soyuz-TMA flight engineer and qualified mission specialist for NASA. She was a mission specialist for *Discovery* STS-131 in 2010, operating the remote manipulator systems of both the shuttle and the space station. She was also loadmaster of cargo transfer. Naoko later returned to aerospace engineering and working for JAXA until retiring in August 2011.

Chiaki is currently the head of the JAXA Space Biomedical Research Office. Published in more than 60 publications in her lifetime, she has won honors and recognition in the United States as well as in Japan. On one of her early spaceflights, she said she hoped her flights into space would encourage other Japanese women to do things they might hesitate to do because they are women.[4]

LEARN MORE

"Chiaki Mukai." NASA. http://spaceflight.nasa.gov/shuttle /archives/sts-95/crew/mukai.html.

Emerging Space Powers: The New Space Programs of Asia, the Middle East and South-America by Bran Harvey, Henk H. F. Smid, and Theo Pirard. (Springer Praxis Books, 2010).

The Space Shuttle: Celebrating Thirty Years of NASA's First Space Plane by Piers Bizony (Zenith Press, 2011).

CLAUDIE ANDRÉ-DESHAYS HAIGNERÉ

· · · · · · · · · · · · · ·

FRENCH ASTRONAUT AND
SOYUZ COMMANDER

Several women around the world found that the path to becoming an astronaut started with becoming a physician. The first women astronauts from Canada and Japan were physicians. So was the first female European astronaut, Claudie Haigneré of France. As a physician, she was experienced in rheumatology, sports medicine, and space medicine. She also made two journeys into space with the Russian space program

Commander Victor Afanasyev, flight engineer Konstantin Kozeev, and French flight engineer **Claudie Haigneré** (clockwise from top) wave from a Soyuz spacecraft docked at the International Space Station. *NASA*

and became the first female of any country to qualify as commander of a Soyuz capsule.

According to Claudie, she first began to think about going to space when Neil Armstrong walked on the moon when she was 12 years old. "For me, it was a kind of revelation. I was watching a dream turn into reality. A door was open. I didn't immediately imagine that it was open for me, but the lunar landing gave me a taste for space."[1]

Although Claudie decided to become a doctor, she never forgot that taste of space. As a physician, she became interested in how space affects the human body.

Before becoming an astronaut, Claudie worked in the rheumatology clinic and the rehabilitation department at Cochin Hospital in Paris. Her research applied diagnostic and therapeutic techniques to arthritis and traumatic sports injuries. She later turned her attention to studying the nervous system in the field of neurosensory physiology.

In 1985, the French space agency (*Centre national d'études spatiales*, CNES) chose Claudie to be an astronaut. She took part in astronaut training, including regular parabolic campaigns, which are low-gravity flights that test people and instruments before spaceflights. Parabolic flights are conducted on special aircraft configured for microgravity—in Claudie's case, the Caravelle Zero-G. Usually, a parabolic campaign is three flights, with each flight containing about 30 parabolas, special curved flight paths that mimic reduced gravity (followed by increased gravity), each for about 20 seconds. If a person can't handle a parabolic flight, they can't handle spaceflight.

Like many astronauts, she served as the backup for other astronauts. Astronauts who are backups participate in the same training as the primary astronauts. Claudie was backup in 1992 to Jean-Pierre Haigneré for the Altair mission to the *Mir* station, which would take place during the first three weeks of July 1993. Although she didn't launch with the mission, she did monitor the biomedical experiments at the mission control center in Kaliningrad, Russia.

In the early 1990s, Claudie oversaw international space physiology and medicine programs for the French space agency. She put her medical and scientific skills to work by first coordinating life science experiments on the French-Russian Antares mission in 1992. She also coordinated experiments for other missions, such as the Cassiopée and Euromir 1994 missions.

At the end of 1994, she received news that she was appointed the research cosmonaut for the Cassiopée space science mission. Training started at Star City on January 1 for the mission to *Mir*. It would be the first manned flight using the Soyuz-U booster, although the system had failed on two unmanned flights.

After a successful launch on August 17, 1996, the *Soyuz* TM-24 docked with *Mir* two days later. Claudie worked on life science experiments, particularly physiology, developmental biology, and fluid physics. She collected a significant amount of data, which she shared with the scientific community upon her return from the 16-day flight.

She was again appointed as backup for Jean-Pierre Haigneré for the Perseus mission to the *Mir* Space Station in February 1999. This was one of several French-Russian spaceflights. After serving as backup for Haigneré twice, Claudie married him two years later.

During training for the Perseus mission, Claudie became qualified as cosmonaut engineer for both the Soyuz vehicle and the *Mir* Space Station. This meant that she could serve as commander of a Soyuz capsule upon a return flight. Although she never had the opportunity to use the certification, achieving it was quite an accomplishment because it was a difficult certification to earn. She also received EVA training. When the Perseus mission launched in February 1999, Claudie served as crew interface coordinator at Mission Control.

On her second flight in October 2001, Claudie was able to apply her physiology training to research weightlessness during her eight-day stay. Specifically, she studied how the motor and cognitive systems adapted to weightlessness.

After the mission, Claudie joined the European Space Agency's European Astronaut Corps, based in Cologne, Germany. She was appointed to work on development projects and medical support for the microgravity facilities. She then got the

The European Space Agency

With its headquarters in Paris, the European Space Agency (ESA) has offices throughout Europe, including Spain, Italy, the Netherlands, and the United Kingdom. The astronauts' office is in Cologne, Germany. The ESA also has liaison offices and tracking stations throughout the world. So which countries are in the ESA?

Austria	Belgium	Czech Republic
Denmark	Finland	France
Germany	Greece	Ireland
Italy	Luxembourg	Netherlands
Norway	Poland	Portugal
Romania	Spain	Sweden
Switzerland	United Kingdom	

opportunity to go into space again and began training in Russia for the Andromeda mission to the International Space Station (ISS). She was Europe's first female at the ISS and the first person from France. She was the second astronaut from the ESA at the station. At the time, she was also the only woman astronaut in the ESA.

On October 21, 2001, Claudie served as Soyuz flight engineer in what was called the "first taxi flight" to the ISS, where Shannon Lucid was stationed. The Andromeda mission had two main tasks. They would switch out the Soyuz crew escape vehicle, and they would carry out scientific and medical research

Europe Getting Ready for Women on Mars

The European Space Agency is experimenting with 24 women on Earth to prepare for the day that women astronauts will go to the neighboring planet of Mars. Women from eight European countries participated in the Women International Space Simulation for Exploration (WISE) campaign. The experiment required the women to stay in bed for 60 days and complete all activities with their heads about six degrees below horizontal. This position results in physiological changes in the body that are similar to those experienced in weightlessness. The experiment also looked at the roles of nutrition and exercise in counteracting adverse conditions that arise from being in low-gravity situations for extended periods of time, such as when astronauts go to other planets.

organized by the French space agency. Claudie felt it was important to get the laboratories running and show European children that Europe was an important part of space exploration and research.

Claudie's work with the Russian space program is said to have been a strong factor in the good working relationship between France and Russia. She has been recognized by both her home country and Russia. From Russia, she received the Order of Friendship and Medal for Personal Valour.

Now a retired astronaut, Claudie has remained active in government, serving as minister for research and new technologies and later as minister for European affairs and secretary general for Franco-German cooperation. But space exploration is never far from her heart. Claudie left her government posts in November 2005 to return to work for the European Space Agency. As adviser to the director general, she works on European space policy.

LEARN MORE

"Claudie Haigneré (formerly André-Deshays)." European Space Agency. www.esa.int/esaHS/M8AVCKSC_astronauts_0.html.

"Expedition Three Crew." NASA. http://spaceflight.nasa.gov/station/crew/exp3/taxi3/haignere.html.

Space Odyssey: The First Forty Years of Space Exploration by Serge Brunier and Stephen Lyle (Cambridge University Press, 2002).

YI SOYEON

FIRST FROM KOREA

Some women were not only the first women in space from their countries, they were the first people—male or female—from their countries to go to space. Helen Sharman of Great Britain and Anousheh Ansari of Iran were the first people from their countries to achieve spaceflight. Another was Yi Soyeon from South Korea. (Her name sometimes appears as So-yeon Yi.)

As spaceflights became more frequent, the costs became staggering, as the United States and Russia have learned. According to NASA, each space shuttle mission costs in the neighborhood of $450 million. Russia's answer to soaring costs was to sell spaceflights to various countries. These countries, eager to

---

Yi Soyeon, Yuri Malenchenko, and Peggy Whitson (from left to right) in the *Harmony* node of the International Space Station. *NASA*

put someone into space, paid the price. That person then went through training at Star City. In addition to Great Britain, countries such as Afghanistan, Mongolia, and Vietnam were part of this project. South Korea became the 35th county in space in 2007. The bill to send a South Korean into space came to $20 million.

In 2006, SouthKorea began taking applications for its first astronaut. With approximately 36,000 applicants, it took until Christmas of that year to choose two finalists: Ko San, a roboticist and computer engineer, and Yi Soyeon, a bioengineer.

For Yi Soyeon, it was a dream come true. She remembered watching science fiction movies as a child. When the cool astronauts flew in their spaceships, there was always one female, a scientist. That female scientist was always smart, and if something happened, she always explained everything well.[1]

According to Soyeon, she was no different than other South Korean kids pretending to fly into space. But deep down, they all knew that the only ones to get jobs as astronauts were Americans or Russians. Now she hopes her experience will keep other Korean children believing that they can go to space, too.

With a master's degree in engineering from the Korea Advanced Institute of Science and Technology (South Korea's first research-oriented science and engineering institution), Soyeon wanted to be one of those cool astronauts, so she took off for training in Russia with Ko San.

One of the hardest things about training was learning to speak and understand Russian. Soyeon worked very hard, but in September 2007, the Korean Ministry of Science and Technology chose Ko San as the primary astronaut. Soyeon would be the backup.

Training began for a 2008 spaceflight to the International Space Station on a Soyuz spacecraft. Suddenly, on March 7,

Soyeon moved from backup to training with the primary crew instead of Ko San. Three days later, South Korea's Ministry of Education, Science, and Technology announced that Soyeon would replace San on the flight.

Russia's Federal Space Agency asked that San be replaced after repeated violations of regulations. He reportedly removed sensitive materials and sent them to Korea. One item was a training manual. He also had a book in his possession that he wasn't meant to read.

On April 8, 2008, Soyeon was launched on *Soyuz* TMA-12 at the age of 29. She flew with two cosmonauts to the International Space Station where she spent approximately a week conducting many scientific experiments. She felt it was important that she do a good job in representing South Korea.

The Russian Soyuz TMA spacecraft was the first spacecraft to take a crew to the International Space Station. Additionally, a Soyuz ship is kept at the space station in case the crew needs to return to Earth unexpectedly.

After almost 11 days in space, Soyeon returned on *Soyuz* TMA-11 with the 16th group of long-duration crew. The crew included Russian cosmonaut Yuri Malenchenko and American astronaut Dr. Peggy Whitson, both of whom had just finished six-month rotations at the space station. Whitson had just completed her tour as commander of the space station, as well.

The Soyuz capsule landed 260 miles off its targeted landing site in Kazakhstan because of a steep reentry or ballistic descent that caused burning to the hatch and the antenna. Unlike space shuttles that land on Earth like airplanes, Soyuz spacecraft use a parachute and three small engines to slow the capsule for landing. This time, however, the capsule hit the ground so hard that it bounced. All three astronauts were fine, but they looked tired when they emerged from inside.

Soyeon had a big smile on her face. Through an interpreter, she said she would love to go to space again, particularly on a long-duration mission. Since returning, Soyeon has worked as a senior scientific researcher, but she also spends a lot of time as a "space ambassador" for her country. In this role, she travels and speaks to the public and at schools. Immediately after her flight, she spoke at schools almost daily; about four years later, her speaking engagements decreased to approximately one each week.

LEARN MORE

Asia's Space Race: National Motivations, Regional Rivalries, and International Risks by James Clay Moltz (Columbia University Press, 2011).

"International Brief: Dr. Soyeon Yi." NASA. www.nasa .gov/offices/oce/appel/ask-academy/issues/volume5 /5-5_dr_soyeon_yi.html.

KALPANA CHAWLA

· · · · · · · · · · · · · ·

A TRAGIC END

An aeronautical engineer from India, Kalpana Chawla took her first flight in 1996 as a mission specialist and primary robotic arm operator for STS-87. It was the fourth of NASA's microgravity payload flights. A strong focus of the mission was studying how the extremely low gravity in space affected humans. The crew also studied the sun's outer atmosphere and tested EVA tools for use on the International Space Station.

One particular moment in space that meant a lot to her was just a reflection in the overhead window of the spacecraft, but it was a powerful image. "I could then see my reflection in the window and in the retina of my eyes the whole earth and the

---

Mission specialist **Kalpana Chawla** works with the Microgravity Payload-4 glovebox on Mission STS-87. *NASA*

sky could be seen reflected. . . . So I called all the crew members one by one and they all saw it and everybody said, "Oh . . . wow."[1]

As the spacecraft returned to Earth, Kalpana was able to see the Himalayas and the majestic Ganges Valley of India and her home near New Delhi, which she pointed out to fellow crew members. Kalpana was the first woman from India and the continent of Asia to go into space. She became a hero in her native India, a country that had launched satellites and hoped to orbit the moon someday.

Born in Karnal, India, Kalpana was the youngest of four children. She was also the third daughter in a country that prized the birth of sons more, but this only fueled her drive to succeed. She also came from a family with strong drive. Her parents had moved from Pakistan to India with very little, but her father was determined to make it and became a successful rubber industrialist. Like many Pakistani fathers, Kalpana's father believed his daughter's role was submissive to that of her family and future husband, but Kalpana's mother supported her daughter's dream of education and independence.

Kalpana left home to attend Punjab Engineering College with her brother. She was the only woman to major in aeronautical engineering. People tried to talk her out of it, but she was determined and received a bachelor of science degree in aeronautical engineering. She took up flying planes, inspired by J. R. D. Tata, a pilot who flew the first mail flights in India. Kalpana loved flying, whether it was in space or closer to the Earth. She held glider and instrument ratings, plus commercial pilot licenses for single-engine and multiengine aircraft and seaplanes. She particularly enjoyed aerobatics (doing stunts in the air).

She moved to the United States to continue her education, first at the University of Texas, where she earned a master of science degree, and then at the University of Colorado, where she earned a PhD in aeronautical engineering.

After receiving her PhD, Kalpana went to work at NASA's Ames Research Center. Her first project was on powered-lift computational fluid dynamics. Afterward, she took that knowledge and applied the research to mapping flow solvers to parallel computers.

Five years later, Kalpana was working with a private company in the aeronautical industry. She led a team of researchers in developing techniques for improving aerodynamics. Following completion of this project, she researched, developed, and tested powered lift computations. Results of various projects that she participated in were documented in technical conference papers and journals.

Refusing her country's tradition of arranged marriages, she chose her husband in the United States and became an American citizen. There was tension with her family for a while because of her decision, but when she joined the space program, they grew closer again. The Chawlas were very proud of Kalpana.

In 1994, Kalpana began astronaut training at Johnson Space Center. As part of the 15th group of astronauts, she was assigned to technical issues for the Astronaut Office EVA/Robotics and Computer Branches after she completed her year of training. She specifically worked on space shuttle control software and Robotic Situational Awareness Displays. After her first flight, Kalpana was appointed the lead for the Astronaut Office's Crew Systems and Habitability section.

Kalpana asked NASA to invite high school students from her school in India to participate in a summer space program that involved the International Space Station. Each year, two students from the high school traveled to Houston to participate in the program at the Johnson Space Center. Kalpana and her husband would feed them Indian food at their home. She told the students, "Whatever you believe in, do—just follow your dreams."[2]

Kalpana's second flight was longer, a 16-day dedicated science and research mission aboard the space shuttle *Columbia*. She and the crew successfully completed 80 experiments during their mission.

Like the rest of the world, India was quite unprepared for the events of February 1, 2003. The space shuttle *Columbia* was coming back into the Earth's atmosphere, only 16 minutes away from landing. Flying approximately 40 miles over central Texas, the shuttle was going to land at Kennedy Space Center in Florida. When spacecraft reenter the Earth's atmosphere, temperatures can reach as high as 3,000 degrees Fahrenheit, so the shuttle trajectory or flight path is calculated to minimize problems from the heat.

Everything appeared to be normal upon reentry, but then at 7:53 AM Central Time, Mission Control in Houston noted a sensor for the left-side hydraulic system falling to zero as a 60-degree spike was recorded between the tiles along the fuselage. Another temperature sensor failed minutes later. Then communication was lost.

As the *Columbia* slowed down, it began to break apart, killing the seven crewmembers instantly. Also part of the crew was mission specialist Laurel Blair Salton Clark.

Investigators and NASA personnel raked through the debris strewn over a 900-square-mile area in East Texas and Louisiana. The *Columbia* had been the oldest operational space shuttle, flying on its 28th mission. NASA engineers began reviewing footage. Foam insulation was observed falling off the shuttle's left tank during the launch weeks earlier.

Within a couple days, NASA announced that increased temperatures affected the left exterior side of the shuttle where a

Laurel Blair Salton Clark

••

Columbia Mission STS-107 was the first spaceflight for physician Laurel Blair Salton Clark, picked for astronaut training in 1996. She came to NASA as a US Navy commander and naval flight surgeon. After training, she worked in the Astronaut Office Payloads/Habitability Branch until she was named a mission specialist for Mission STS-107. Her husband, former NASA flight surgeon Dr. Jonathan Clark, worked on the *Columbia* investigation.

tile may have been missing or damaged. Officials hoped to gain access to another 32 seconds of computer data after communication with the shuttle failed.

As before, NASA halted scheduled shuttle flights until the cause could be determined and fixed. Unlike at the time of the *Challenger* disaster, this time three people remained on the International Space Station—a Russian cosmonaut and two American astronauts. They had been scheduled to be picked up by the *Atlantis* a month later.

Investigators issued a 400-page report of their findings. The crew did everything they were supposed to do. Nothing could have saved them from the problems upon reentry, so the only thing to do to prevent the tragedy from reoccurring was to prevent problems on reentry. It was determined that the insulating foam had punched a hole in the left wing, which allowed the gasses to overheat during reentry. The result was described as a blowtorch. The foam that caused the problem weighed only 1.67 pounds.

NASA redesigned the external fuel tank and reduced the amount of foam used. New pressure suits and helmets were part of the redesign as well.

After her death, Dr. Kalpana Chawla was awarded NASA's Distinguished Service Medal and Space Flight Medal in addition to the Congressional Space Medal of Honor.

LEARN MORE

Disasters in Space Exploration (Revised Edition) by Gregory Vogt (21st Century, 2003).

"Space Shuttle *Columbia* and Her Crew." NASA. www.nasa .gov/columbia/crew/profile_kalpanac.html.

LIU YANG

····················

FLYING KNIGHT IN SPACE

The Chinese people had plenty to celebrate in late June and early July 2012. The third country into space, China launched the *Shenzhou 9* spacecraft from the Jiuquan Satellite Launch Center in China's Gobi Desert. Three astronauts were on board, one of whom was making his second flight into space. The youngest member of the three-person crew was China's first woman in space, 33-year-old Liu Yang, an air force pilot and major.

While that was exciting, another first for China's busy space program was that this mission included the first manned docking with the *Tiangong* space module, launched into space in

---

Liu Yang visiting the Chinese University of Hong Kong in 2012. She has been much in demand as a speaker since returning from space. *Tksteven (Wikipedia commons)*

September 2011. *Tiangong* is the beginning of China's planned space station, which is expected to be completed by 2020. The docking was performed with hand levers. The *Shenzhou 9* crew was also the first to live on the *Tiangong 1*.

The 13-day mission was China's first manned flight since 2008. Yang worked on medical experiments in the *Tiangong* module. With a new perspective on the size of the universe, Yang believes there must be other life out there. However, while in space, the crew of the *Shenzhou 9* sent greetings to closer space travelers, those at the International Space Station.

The landing of the *Shenzhou* capsule in Inner Mongolia was also televised. Soon after it entered the Earth's atmosphere, a huge striped parachute shot up as the capsule gently swayed in the air. After touching down, Yang came out of the capsule smiling and waving. "It is a very different experience up in the air. When you look back to your homeland, you get caught up with a surge of emotions within you."[1]

Yang's enthusiasm for space was obvious, whether she was talking to the media, the public, or fellow professionals. With a ready smile, she responded well to the media attention both before and after her flight, an aspect of the role that many astronauts dread. In an early public appearance, she said, "Every minute in space, I felt like a fish that swims in water freely. Everything floats and flies because of the weightlessness. Compared with the Earth, it seems that everything in space has got a life."[2]

Yang, originally from the central province of Henan, joined the army in 1997. Being a pilot wasn't her first career choice. As a child, she thought she might be either a lawyer or a bus driver, although becoming a female martial arts heroine like the kind she watched on TV sounded like fun, too.

When training with transport planes, she soon earned a reputation for staying cool under pressure—even when, for example, one of the engines on her plane stopped working in the air after it collided with birds. With more than 1,680 flying hours, she was given the flight name Little Flying Knight.

Recruited by China's space agency in 2010, she excelled in the training and was an obvious choice to be the ninth Chinese astronaut sent into space. Millions watched the live launch, powered by a Long March 2F rocket, on China Central Television.

Although China is late to the Space Race, it has progressed much more quickly than either the United States or Russia. The first space walk for China was in 2008, only five years after their first manned spaceflight. The manual docking was another step in their progression. Seven months earlier, the China's space agency had performed an automatic docking from their control center in Beijing. Other plans include sending a Chinese astronaut to the moon within a few years.

Unlike the United States, China uses both military and civilian resources in its space program. It already had experience with launching satellites into space before it began its manned

China Wants to Grow Vegetables on the Moon

In December 2012, the China Space Agency released plans for building a greenhouse on the moon. After experimenting with the plan on Earth, officials believe that having greenhouses as part of future bases would supply astronauts with vegetables and another source of oxygen. The plants would also take in carbon dioxide, which can be harmful to humans in large amounts.

space program and has since spent billions of dollars on the program.

All three astronauts of the *Shenzhou 9* mission were recognized by their country with medals. Yang has also been honored by the All-China Women's Federation. She and her husband now live in Beijing, the capital of China. It's been rumored that Yang will get another opportunity to return to space, something she welcomes and continues training for. Yang and other astronauts perform the Chinese meditative and physical exercise tai chi both on Earth and in space. Yang wants to be ready for future missions if called for them.

Meanwhile, Yang advises wannabe astronauts to exercise regularly and stay healthy. She particularly encourages Chinese women and girls to participate in the program.

LEARN MORE

"The Future of US-China Space Cooperation." NASA. www.nasa.gov/offices/oce/appel/ask-academy/issues /ask-oce/AO_1-10_F_future.html.

"Profile of Liu Yang, China's First Woman Astronaut." BBC News. www.bbc.co.uk/news/science-environment -18471236.

SAMANTHA CRISTOFORETTI

•••••••••••••

MILITARY PILOT ASTRONAUT

Soon after you read this, there might be an Italian woman in space. That's what Samantha Cristoforetti of Milan is training for right now. Her flight to the International Space Station (ISS) has been scheduled for 2014. She is to launch in a Soyuz spacecraft from the Baikonur Cosmodrome in Kazakhstan as part of Expedition 42/43. Within two days, she will step inside the ISS for a six-month stay. She will be the eighth ESA astronaut to go to the ISS for a long assignment.

Italy is not a large country, so perhaps it isn't too surprising that Samantha is the first female astronaut from her country. A little more surprising is that in more than 50 years of spaceflights,

European Space Agency astronaut **Samantha Cristoforetti** trains for Expedition 42/43 as the flight engineer. The expedition is scheduled for 2014. *NASA*

she is only the third female astronaut from the European Space Agency. The first was physician Claudie Haigneré from France. The second was Marianne Merchez, a physician who hails from Belgium and specializes in space medicine. Marianne never flew in space, though. She resigned after three years and returned to practicing medicine.

The ESA astronaut candidate classes and frequency are quite limited. There have only been three classes of astronauts from the European Space Agency compared to 20 in the United States. Claudie and Marianne were from the first class, in 1992. Samantha is from the most recent one, in 2009. Samantha is the only woman among the 15 active astronauts in the ESA in 2012.

Samantha isn't a physician. She is an engineer and a military pilot. A captain in the Italian Air Force, she has more than 500 hours of military flight experience on six types of military jets.

To prepare for space and a stay at the space station, Samantha is training in the United States, Russia, Germany, and Japan. Training includes learning about Soyuz spacecraft and ISS systems in addition to robotics and extravehicular training for spacewalks.

Samantha completed secondary school at Liceo Scintifico after spending a year in the United States as an exchange student. She has a degree in aeronautical engineering from the University of Munich. She continued her education in Munich and Moscow, earning a master's degree in mechanical engineering with specializations in aerospace propulsion and lightweight structures. During her education, she focused on aerodynamics and wrote her thesis on solid rocket propellants.

Samantha also graduated from the Italian Air Force Academy in 2005, earning her military pilot wings the next year. One of her first tours of service was at Sheppard Air Force Base in Texas. She received Euro-NATO Joint Jet Pilot training. She flew the MB-339, and as a fighter pilot was assigned to the 132nd Squadron, 51st Bomber Wing, based in Italy. Later, she was reassigned to the 101st Squadron, 32nd Bomber Wing with training for the AMX ground-attack fighter. In 2009, she was chosen for astronaut training.

LEARN MORE

"Samantha Cristoforetti." European Space Agency. www .esa.int/esaHS/SEMHZJ0OWUF_astronauts_0.html.

Samantha Cristoforetti photo. NASA. http://spaceflight .nasa.gov/gallery/images/station/crew-42/html/jsc 2012e237644.html.

THE FUTURE OF SPACEFLIGHT

••••••••••••••••

Just like space itself, the future of spaceflight is wide open. Commercial companies like SpaceX are ready to fill the void that the ending of the US space shuttle program left. In both May and October 2012, the *Dragon* cargo spacecraft successfully made supply runs to the International Space Station, completing 2 of the 12 unmanned Commercial Resupply Services flights that SpaceX was contracted by NASA to carry out. The *Dragon* brings approximately a thousand pounds of supplies, including materials for experiments. When the *Dragon* gets close to the space station, crewmembers use the station's arm to grab the supply ship and place it in the port near the *Harmony* module. Once the *Dragon* is docked, ISS crewmembers unload the supplies before reloading the cargo ship with results of scientific experiments and other items not needed by the ISS.

NASA will continue with unmanned scientific exploration projects, for now. Initial success with exploring Mars, our nearest neighbor, will continue with seven missions. Other countries are expanding their space programs with missions, as well.

Within the next 10 years, there will most likely be ships orbiting Mars and landing on the moon again.

Expeditions to the ISS will also continue. Astronaut Karen Nyberg has been the most recent woman in space, serving as flight engineer for Expedition 36 and 37.

NASA has recently selected its 2013 astronaut class. Of the eight trainees, half are women. Women in space are women of courage who are committed to exploration and knowledge.

ACKNOWLEDGMENTS

....

A huge thank you to Martha Ackmann, whose book, *The Mercury 13: The True Story of Thirteen Women and the Dream of Space Flight,* continues to inspire me every time I open its pages. I couldn't have undertaken this project without the amazing collection of information about missions, spacecraft, and astronauts at NASA. I hope the Women@NASA website continues to grow and that space exploration will begin its new chapter soon. And thank you to the great people at Chicago Review Press, who make it so easy to write what I love.

ACKNOWLEDGMENTS

NOTES

....

INTRODUCTION

1. National Aeronautics and Space Act of 1958, http://history.nasa
   .gov/spaceact.html.
2. "Women of Aviation Worldwide Week," www.womenofaviation
   week.org.

PART I: THE MERCURY 13

1. "Mercury 13: University of Wisconsin, Oshkosh," www.uwosh
   .edu/mercury13/.
2. James Oberg, "The Mercury 13: Setting the Story Straight," *Space
   Review*, www.thespacereview.com/article/869/1.
3. *Honoring the Mercury 13 Women*, 110 Cong. Rec. H6020 (2007),
   http://thomas.loc.gov/cgi-bin/query/R?r110:FLD001:H06020.

The Astronauts Who Never Were

1. Stephanie Nolen, *Promised the Moon: The Untold Story of the First
   Women in Space* (Toronto, ON: Penguin Canada, 2002), 89.
2. Jerrie Cobb with Jane Rieker, *Woman into Space: The Jerrie Cobb
   Story* (Englewood Cliffs, NY: Prentice-Hall, 1963), 1.

3. Nolen, *Promised the Moon*, 93–94.
4. Margaret A. Weitekamp, *Right Stuff, Wrong Sex: America's First Women in Space Program* (Baltimore: Johns Hopkins University Press, 2004), 77.
5. Martha Ackmann, *The Mercury 13: The True Story of Thirteen Women and the Dream of Space Flight* (New York: Random House, 2004).
6. Cobb and Rieker, *Woman Into Space*.
7. "Mercury 13 – The Secret Astronauts," YouTube video, posted by TheMercuryChannel. December 15, 2008. http://www.youtube .com/watch?v=WWySNMbGz0w.
8. Cobb and Rieker, *Woman into Space*.
9. Ackmann, *The Mercury 13*.
10. Weitekamp, *Right Stuff, Wrong Sex*, 117.
11. Ackmann, *The Mercury 13*.
12. "Woman Astronaut Predicted," *New York Times*, June 26, 1962.
13. "Honoring the Mercury 13 Women," University of Wisconsin–Oshkosh, panel discussion, iTunes U podcast, part 2. May 11, 2007.
14. *Qualifications for Astronauts, Hearings before the United States House Committee on Science and Astronautics, Special Subcommittee on the Selection of Astronauts*, 87th Cong., second session, (July 17–18, 1962).
15. *Qualifications for Astronauts*.
16. Nolen, *Promised the Moon*, 272.
17. Bettyann Holtzmann Kevles, *Almost Heaven: The Story of Women in Space* (New York: Basic Books, 2006), 42–43.

PART II: COSMONAUTS

1. "I See Earth! It Is So Beautiful!," European Space Agency, www.esa .int/esaCP/SEM5A57S9MG_index_0.html.
2. David J. Shayler and Ian A. Moule, *Women in Space: Following Valentina* (UK: Praxis Publishing, 2005), 45.
3. James Oberg, "Does Mars Need Women? Russians Say No," NBC News, February 11, 2005, http://msnbc.msn.com/id/6955149/.

Valentina Tereshkova: First in Space

1. Nolen, *Promised the Moon*, 191.
2. Shayler and Moule, *Women in Space*.
3. Shayler and Moule, *Women in Space*, 106.

Svetlana Savitskaya: No Apron for Her

1. John F. Burns, "An Apron for Soviet Woman in Space," *New York Times*, August 29, 1982.
2. Burns, "An Apron for Soviet Woman."
3. Seth Mydans, "Female Soviet Astronaut Says That Women Have a Place in Space," *New York Times*, August 11, 1984.

PART III: AMERICAN WOMEN JOIN THE SPACE RACE

1. Madeline Novey, "Former NASA Astronaut, Alumna Returns to Colorado State," *Fort Collins Coloradoan*, October 5, 2012.
2. Sarah Harmon, "Astronaut to Speak at Women in Technology Conference," *Intelligencer, Wheeling News-Register*, October 11, 2012.

Sally Ride: First American Woman in Space

1. Michelle Mowad, "Sally Ride—First American Woman in Space," *LaJolla Patch*, July 23, 2012, http://lajolla.patch.com/articles/sally -ride-first-american-woman-in-space-dies-in-la-jolla.
2. Rick Hauck, "Memories of My Space Flight with Sally Ride," *Lightyears* (blog), http://lightyears.blogs.cnn.com/2012/07/24 /memories-of-my-space-flight-with-sally-ride/.
3. Scott Herhold, "The Day Sally Ride Was Picked for Astronaut Training," *San Jose Mercury News*, July 23, 2012.
4. "Biography," Sally Ride Science. www.sallyridescience.com /sallyride/bio.
5. "A Chat with Sally Ride," *Time for Kids*, www.timeforkids.com /news/chat-sally-ride/10901.
6. Eyder Peralta, "Sally Ride, First Woman in Space, Is Dead" WNYC News, July 23, 2012, www.wnyc.org/npr_articles/2012/jul/23 /sally-ride-first-american-woman-in-space-is-dead/.

7. Kathryn Sullivan, "The Human, Funny Side of Sally Ride," CNN, http://www.cnn.com/2012/07/24/opinion/sullivan-sally-ride/index.html?iref=allsearch.

8. Associated Press, "America's First Female Astronaut Sally Ride Dies," July 23, 2012. http://www.foxnews.com/scitech/2012/07/23/america-first-female-astronaut-sally-ride-dies.

9. Associated Press, "America's First Female Astronaut."

10. Associated Press, "America's First Female Astronaut."

Judith Resnik: All She Ever Wanted to Do

1. Seymour Brody, "Judith Resnik," Jewish Virtual Library, www.jewishvirtuallibrary.org/jsource/biography/Resnik.html.

2. Brody, "Judith Resnik."

3. Brody, "Judith Resnik."

Kathryn Sullivan: A Walk into History

1. William J. Broad, "'Really Great,' Says the First Woman from US to Take a Walk in Space," *New York Times*, October 12, 1984.

2. Broad, "'Really Great.'"

Shannon Lucid: A Russian Favorite

1. "NASA-2 Shannon Lucid: Enduring Qualities," NASA, http://history.nasa.gov/SP-4225/nasa2/nasa2.htm.

2. "NASA-2 Shannon Lucid."

Mae Jemison: Doctor Astronaut

1. Warren E. Leary, "Woman in the News: A Determined Breaker of Boundaries—Mae Carol Jemison," *New York Times*, September 13, 1992.

2. "Campus Journal; For a Black Woman, Space Isn't the Final Frontier," *New York Times*, March 3, 1993.

3. Nadine Brozan, "Chronicle," *New York Times*, September 16, 1992.

4. "FAQs," *Dr. Mae*, www.drmae.com/faqs-100.

5. Leary, "Woman in the News."

6. "Campus Journal."

Eileen Collins: Space Shuttle Commander

1. John Schwartz, "To Revive Shuttle, NASA Calls on a Cool Leader," *New York Times* Learning Network, April 18, 2005, www.nytimes .com/learning/teachers/featured_articles/20050418monday .html.

Pamela Melroy: Piloting in Space

1. John Schwartz, "Amid Concerns, an Ambitious Shuttle Mission," *New York Times*, October 21, 2007.
2. Schwartz, "Amid Concerns."
3. Kenneth Chang, "With 'Coolest Job Ever' Ending, Astronauts Seek Next Frontier," *New York Times*, April 23, 2011.

Peggy Whitson: Space Station Commander

1. Ann Parson, "Scientist at Work, Peggy Whitson Testing Limits, 220 Miles Above Earth," *New York Times*, September 5, 2006.
2. Alyssa Miller, "Astronaut Peggy Whitson Visits Science Center of Iowa," *Iowa State Daily*, October 12, 2012.
3. "A Desk Job Just Wasn't for Astronaut Peggy Whitson," *Des Moines Register*, October 12, 2012.
4. Parson, "Scientist at Work."
5. Parson, "Scientist at Work."
6. Parson, "Scientist at Work."
7. Chang, "With 'Coolest Job Ever.'"

Sunita Williams: Breaking Records

1. Todd Halvorson, "Spacewalkers Fix Electrical Feed During Record-Setting ISS Outing," *Florida Today*, www.floridatoday .com/article/20120905/SPACE/120905009/U-S-astronaut-Suni -Williams-sets-spacewalking-record?nclick_check=1.
2. "Astronaut Suni Williams Talks Dessert, Voting and Triathlons from Space," ABC News, http://abcnews.go.com/blogs/tech nology/2012/10/astronaut-suni-williams-talks-dessert-voting-and -triathlons-from-space/.

3. Denise Chow, "Space Triathlon: Station Astronaut to Compete Where No One Has Before," *Space.com*, August 14, 2012, www.space.com/17092-space-triathlon-station-astronaut-sunita-williams.html.

Barbara Morgan: Teachers in Space

1. Kenneth Chang, "Shuttle *Endeavour* Lifts Off Toward Space Station," *New York Times*, August 9, 2007.
2. Warren E. Leary, "Teacher-Astronaut to Fly Decades After *Challenger*," *New York Times*, August 7, 2007.
3. "Barbara Morgan: No Limits." Marcia Franklin, Producer. Idaho Public Television. video.idahoptv.org
4. "Barbara Morgan: No Limits."
5. "Barbara Morgan: No Limits."

PART IV: WORLD ASTRONAUTS

1. "1991: Sharman Becomes First Briton in Space," *On This Day*, BBC News, http://news.bbc.co.uk/onthisday/hi/dates/stories/may/18/newsid_2380000/2380649.stm.

Roberta Bondar: Living a Childhood Dream

1. "The Making of Dreams," Dr. Roberta Bondar website, www.robertabondar.com/astronaut.php.

Chiaki Mukai: Opening Doors

1. Warren E. Leary, "Space Shuttle to Explore Low-Gravity Effects," *New York Times*, July 8, 1994.
2. "Space Aging," *Online News Hour*, PBS, October 29, 1998, www.pbs.org/newshour/bb/science/july-dec98/glenn_10-29.html.
3. Claudia Herrera Hudson, "Explorer Hero: Chiaki Mukai," www.myhero.com/go/print.asp?hero=JapanChiakiMukai.
4. Warren E. Leary, "Newts and Metal Projects Ride *Columbia* into Space," *New York Times*, July 9, 1994.

Claudie André-Deshays Haigneré: French Astronaut and Soyuz Commander

1. "An Interview with Claudie Haigneré," European Space Agency, www.esa.int/esaHS/ESA2CU0VMOC_astronauts_0.html.

Yi Soyeon: First from Korea

1. "First Korean Astronaut Yi So-yeon," *Women in Science* (blog), March 11, 2008, http://blog.sciencewomen.com/2008/03/first -korean-astronaut-yi-so-yeon.html.

Kalpana Chawla: A Tragic End

1. "Kalpana Chawla's Journey," YouTube, http://youtube/3m0NL NDmjE0.
2. Amy Waldman, "LOSS OF THE SHUTTLE: THE CALL OF SPACE; For Resolute Girl, the Traditions of India Imposed No Limits," *New York Times*, February 3, 2003.

Liu Yang: Flying Knight in Space

1. Jasmine Siu, "You're All Stars, Liu Tells Women," *Standard* (Hong Kong), August 20, 2012.
2. "Liu Yang, China's First Female Astronaut," China Daily/Asia News Network, July 15, 2012, www.chinadaily.com.cn/china /Shenzhou-IX/2012-06/15/content_15506101.htm.

GLOSSARY

....

astronautics: The science and technology of spaceflight.

astrophysics: The study of the physical and chemical nature of celestial objects.

burn: Rocket combustion; spacecraft move in space through a sequence of burns.

extravehicular activity: An astronaut or cosmonaut in space outside the spacecraft; a spacewalk.

hatch: Door or doorway, usually sealed airtight.

launch pad: The place from which a rocket or spacecraft is fired.

launch window: The period of time during which a space vehicle can be launched to accomplish a specific mission.

light-year: The distance light travels in one year, approximately 5.88 trillion miles.

lunar: Pertaining to the moon.

magnetic field: An area of space where magnetic forces can be detected.

microgravity: An environment of weak or low gravitational forces.

module: A self-contained unit of a spacecraft or space station; a building block for the total structure.

propulsion: The process of driving movement by means of a chemical mixture that creates the thrust for spacecraft.

payload: Cargo carried by a spacecraft.

radar: The use of radio waves to find out the position, motions, and nature of an object.

radiation: Electromagnetic waves or particles.

radiation belt: An area of high-energy particles trapped in the Earth's magnetic field.

reentry: The descent into Earth's atmosphere from space.

satellite: A natural or artificial body that orbits a planet.

sensor: An electronic device that measures movement or direction.

simulator: A device that acts like equipment or vehicles and provides a practice environment.

solar array: A panel of light-sensitive cells that generate electrical power for a spacecraft in space.

weightlessness: No force of support on your body due to low gravity results in a feeling of lightness.

zero gravity: A condition in which gravity appears to be absent.

ONLINE RESOURCES
FOR FURTHER READING

....

Chandra Observatory: http://chandra.harvard.edu

The Challenger Center: www.challenger.org

Dr. Mae Jemison. Super Scientists: www.energyquest.ca.gov/scientists /jemison.html

Dorothy Jemison Foundation for Excellence: www.jemisonfoundation .org

Ellen Ochoa. Meet Famous Latinos: http://teacher.scholastic.com /activities/hispanic/ochoa.htm

Ellen Ochoa Biography. Hispanic Culture Online: www.hispanic -culture-online.com/ellen-ochoa-biography.html

European Space Agency: www.esa.int

International Women's Air and Space Museum: www.iwasm.org

Japanese Aerospace Exploration Agency: www.jaxa.jp

Johnson Space Center: www.jsc.nasa.gov

Mercury 13: www.mercury13.com

NASA: www.nasa.gov

NASA TV: www.nasa.gov/ntv

Roberta Bondar: www.robertabondar.com

Sally Ride Science: www.sallyridescience.com

Space Station. PBS: www.pbs.org/spacestation

StarChild: A Learning Center for Young Astronomers: http://star child.gsfc.nasa.gov

BIBLIOGRAPHY

....

Materials for young readers

BOOKS

Ackmann, Martha. *The Mercury 13: The True Story of Thirteen Women and the Dream of Space Flight*. New York: Random House, 2004.

Ansari, Anousheh. *My Dream of Stars: From Daughter of Iran to Space Pioneer*. New York: Palgrave/MacMillian, 2010.

*Carlile, Glenda. *Astronauts, Athletes, and Ambassadors: Oklahoma Women from 1950–2007*. Stillwater, OK: New Forums Press, 2007.

Cobb, Jerrie with Jane Rieker. *Woman Into Space: The Jerrie Cobb Story*. Englewood Cliffs, NY: Prentice Hall, 1963.

Gueldenpfennig, Sonia. *Women in Space Who Changed the World*. New York: Rosen Publishing Group, 2010.

Kevles, Bettyann Holtzmann. *Almost Heaven: The Story of Women in Space*. New York: Basic Books, 2007.

Lothian, A. *Valentina: First Woman in Space*. Edinburgh, Scotland: Pentland Press, 1993.

Nolen, Stephanie. *Promised the Moon: The Untold Story of the First Women in Space*. Toronto: Penguin Canada, 2002.

Shayler, David J. and Ian A. Moule. *Women in Space: Following Valentina*. Chichester, UK: Praxis Publishing, 2005.

*Stone, Tanya Lee. *Almost Astronauts: 13 Women Who Dared to Dream*. Somerville, MA: Candlewick Press, 2009.

Weitekamp. Margaret A. *Right Stuff, Wrong Sex: America's First Women in Space*. Baltimore: Johns Hopkins University Press, 2004.

MAGAZINES AND NEWSPAPERS

"2 Women Selected by NASA for Space Shuttle Missions." *New York Times*. September 22, 1983.

"4 Space Veterans and 3 Novices Make Trip." *New York Times*. January 23, 1992.

"6 of America's 8 Women Astronauts Top Fly in '84." *New York Times*. November 19, 1983.

"71 Pilots Recommended as Possible Astronauts." *New York Times*. July 17, 1963.

"Astronauts Wanted; Women, Minorities Are Urged to Apply." *New York Times*. July 8, 1976.

Barboza, David and Kevin Drew. "First Female Astronaut from China Blasts into Space." *New York Times*. June 16, 2012.

Broad, William J. "4-Hour Delay Called for Shuttle Flight as Wind and Balky Bolt Bar Launching." *New York Times*. January 28, 1986.

Broad, William J. "A Hankering for Home." *New York Times*. September 19, 1986.

Broad, William J. "Blasting Off on a Mission for Cosmic Science." *New York Times*. July 13, 1999.

Broad, William J. "7 Astronauts Prepare to Land Today." *New York Times*. October 13, 1984.

Broad, William J. "Shuttle Heads for Rendezvous with Russians." *New York Times*. February 4, 1995.

Broad, William J. "Woman in the News; Cool, Versatile Astronaut: Sally Kristen Ride." *New York Times*. June 19, 1983.

"Excerpts of Conversation on Shuttle." *New York Times*. July 29, 1986.

"Female Astronaut's Visits to Scunthorpe Were Out of This World." *Scunthorpe Telegraph* (UK). August 23, 2012.

"First Woman in Space: Valentina Vladimirovna Tereshkova." *New York Times*. June 17, 1963.

"Headliners; Spacewalker." *New York Times*. July 29, 1984.

Hevesi, Dennis. "Astronaut Takes City Where She Was Raised to the Stars." *New York Times*. February 6, 1995.

"Largest Crew Ever Sent into Space Blends Interest in Flight and Science." *New York Times*. October 6, 1984.

Leary, Warren E. "Astronauts from 3 Countries Ride Shuttle into Orbit." *New York Times*. January 23, 1992.

Leary, Warren E. "International Crew Set for Shuttle Launching." *New York Times*. January 21, 1992.

Leary, Warren E. "Major Component of Space Station Is Attached." *New York Times*. April 12, 2002.

Leary, Warren E. "NASA Official Plays Down a Troubled Soyuz Landing." *New York Times*. April 23, 2008.

Leary, Warren E. "NASA Says 2004 Mission Will Include Schoolteacher." *New York Times*. April 13, 2002.

Leary, Warren E. "Grounded No Longer, Shuttle Atlantis Is Readied for Space." *New York Times*. October 1, 2002.

Leary, Warren E. "Shuttle Crew Plans to Give Space Station Its First Fail Line." *New York Times*. April 2, 2002.

Leary, Warren E. "Shuttle Launched on the Second Try." *New York Times*. April 8, 1993.

Leary, Warren E. "Shuttle Blasts Off for Space Station." *New York Times*. October 8, 2002.

Leary, Warren E. "Space Shuttle Is Launched on 16-Day Science Mission." *New York Times*. October 21, 1995.

Leary, Warren E. "Space Station Awaits Crew with 2 Firsts." *New York Times*. October 11, 2007.

Leary, Warren E. "Space Station Astronauts Report Illnesses." *New York Times*. August 7, 1999.

Leary, Warren E. "US-Japan Mission Is a Shuttle First." *New York Times*. September 13, 1992.

Levine, Richard and Katherine Roberts. "Challenger's Mission Accomplished." *New York Times*. October 14, 1984.

Levine, Richard and Katherine Roberts. "Challenger Takes a Closer Look at Earth." *New York Times*. October 7, 1984.

Mydans, Seth. "Russian Astronaut Becomes First Woman to Walk in Space." *New York Times*. July 26, 1984.

"National News Briefs; Space Shuttle Launching Is Delayed a Second Time." *New York Times.* July 22, 1999.

Navarro, Mireva. "After 6 Months, Her Feet Are Back on the Ground. *New York Times.* September 27, 1996.

Ramirez, Anthony. "Astronauts Are Still Heroes, and Commander Is 'Mom.'" *New York Times.* August 31, 2005.

Revkin, Andrew C. "Now, the Space Station: Grieving, Imperiled." *New York Times.* February 4, 2003.

"Sally Ride Is Willing to Fly." *New York Times.* October 15, 1986.

Sang-Hun, Choe. "Woman Replaces Colleague for South Korea's First Space Mission." *New York Times.* March 11, 2008.

Schwartz, John. "The Astronauts of STS-120." *New York Times.* October 23, 2007.

Schwartz, John. "Astronaut Teaches in Space, and Lesson Is Bittersweet." *New York Times.* August 15, 2007.

Schwartz, John. "Facing and Embracing Risk as Return to Space Nears." *New York Times.* July 10, 2005.

Schwartz, John. "Shuttle Makes Preparations for Risky Return to Earth." *New York Times.* August 7, 2005.

Schwartz, John. "Space Docking with Women at the Helm." *New York Times.* October 26, 2007.

Schwartz, John and William Broad. "Shuttle Glides to Safe Landing; Problems Ahead." *New York Times.* August 10, 2005.

"Soviet Pilot, 34, Becomes Second Woman in Space." *New York Times.* August 20, 1982.

Terry, Dorothy Givens. "Mae Jemison Fights for Diversity in Space and in the Classroom." *Ebony.* September 10, 2012.

"A Thousand Women Inquire About Jobs in Astronaut Corps." *New York Times.* August 27, 1976.

Topping, Seymour. "Soviet Orbits Woman Astronaut Near Bykovsky for Dual Flight; They Talk by Radio, Are Put on TV." *New York Times.* June 17, 1963.

Wilford, John Noble. "A Teacher Trains for Outer Space." *New York Times.* January 5, 1986.

Wilford, John Noble. "First US Woman in Space Called 'Equal' to Men." *New York Times.* July 2, 1983.

Wilford, John Noble. "Risks Were Spelled Out, Shuttle 'Survivor' Says." *New York Times*. April 21, 1986.

Wilford, John Noble. "Teacher Is Picked for Shuttle Trip." *New York Times*. July 20, 1985.

Wines, Michael. "Europe-Moscow: Greetings to Space Station." *New York Times*. October 24, 2001.

Yardley, Jim. "Loss of the Shuttle: The Next Crew; a Shuttle Leader Is Ready 'To Go Fly Again.'" *New York Times*. February 7, 2003.

INTERNET

BBC News. "South Korea swaps first astronaut." http://news.bbc.co.uk/2/hi/7286989.stm.

Block, Melissa. "'The Mercury 13': Training US Women for Space." National Public Radio. June 17, 2003. www.npr.org/2003/06/17/1301400/the-mercury-13-training-u-s-women-for-space.

Christina River Institute. "Pam Melroy." www.christina-river-institute.org/pammelroy/Bio%20&%20Press.htm.

CNN Wire Staff. "China Sends First Female Astronaut to Space." June 16, 2012. www.cnn.com/2012/06/16/world/asia/china-space-launch/index.html.

CTIE. "Svetlana Yevgenyevna Savitskaya (1948–)." Hargrave, The Pioneers. www.ctie.monash.edu.au/hargrave/savitskaya.html.

CTIE. "Yelena Kondakova." Hargrave, The Pioneers. www.ctie.monash.edu.au/hargrave/kondakova.html.

Funk, Wally. "The Mercury 13 Story." The Ninety-Nines, Inc. www.ninety-nines.org/index.cfm/mercury13.htm.

IANS. "Sunita Williams Biography." Bihar Prabha. http://news.biharprabha.com/bp/sunita-williams-biography.

Joshi, Atul. "Biography of Sunita Williams. Real Life Heroine of Space." www.preservearticles.com/201106067543/biography-of-sunita-williams-the-real-heroine-of-space-complete.html.

National Women's Hall of Fame. "Shannon W. Lucid." www.greatwomen.org/component/fabrik/details/2/100.

New Mexico Museum of Space History. "Svetlana Savitskaya." www.nmspacemuseum.org/halloffame/detail.php?id=89.

NOAA. "Dr. Kathryn D. Sullivan." National Ocean and Atmospheric Administration. www.noaa.gov/sullivan.html.

RIA Novosti. "Russian Woman Cosmonaut May Journey to Space Station." Ria Novosti. http://en.rian.ru/world/20111207/169464304 .html.

Schmidt, Klaus. "ESA Astronaut Samantha Cristoforetti Set for Space Station in 2014." Space Fellowship. July 4, 2012. http://spacefellow ship.com/news/art29168/esa-astronaut-samantha-cristoforetti -set-for-space-station-in-2014.html.

Space Today Online. "Teacher-Astronaut Barbara Morgan." www .spacetoday.org/Astronauts/BarbaraMorganTeacherAstronaut .html.

StarChild. "Valentina Tereshkova." http://starchild.gsfc.nasa.gov /docs/StarChild/whos_who_level2/tereshkova.html.

Stuber, Irene. "Capt. Catherine G. Coleman, Ph.D." Women of Achievement and Herstory. www.thelizlibrary.org/collections /woa/woa11-08.html.

Sunseri, Gina. "Discovery Teacher-Astronaut Breaks the Mold." ABC News. http://abcnews.go.com/Technology/dottie-metcalf -lindenburger-astronauts/story?id=10283897.

Women In Military Service For America Memorial Foundation. "Women Part of NASA's 50-year Space Odyssey." www.womens memorial.org/News/NASA50.html.

VIDEO/DVD

A&E Network. "Christa McAuliffe Biography," Biography Channel, www.biography.com/people/christa-mcauliffe-9390406.

Klatell, James M. "Meet the Women of Mercury 13," CBS News, July 15, 2009. www.cbsnews.com/2100-18563_162-2794909.html.

RIA Novosti. "Female Russian Cosmonaut Training for ISS Space Fight." Ria Novosti. http://en.rian.ru/video/20120307/171836165 .html.

Tyson, Peter. "Inside a Spacesuit: Pam Melroy." Nova Online, PBS. www.pbs.org/wgbh/nova/station/media/melroy1.html.

Williams, Brian. "Record-holding Female Spacewalker to Command ISS," NBC Nightly News, September 14, 2012. http://video.msnbc .msn.com/nightly-news/49040191/#49040191.

YOUTUBE

"Challenger Disaster." www.youtube.com/watch?v=j4JOjcDFtBE.

"ESA Astronaut Samantha Cristoforetti Addresses Space Lab Winners." www.youtube.com/watch?v=V639aOYIT4M.

"Mae C. Jemison." www.youtube.com/watch?v=EgOaIKshbIU.

"NASA Television." www.youtube.com/user/NASAtelevision?feature =watch.

"New ESA Astronaut: Samantha Cristoforetti." www.youtube.com /watch?v=k8ser5rZjyU.

INDEX

....